All About Sydney Opera House: A Kid's Guide to Australia's Famous Landmark

Educational Books For Kids, Volume 29

Shah Rukh

Published by Shah Rukh, 2024.

ALL ABOUT SYDNEY OPERA HOUSE: A KID'S GUIDE TO AUSTRALIA'S FAMOUS LANDMARK

First edition. October 14, 2024.

ISBN: 979-8227388056

Written by Shah Rukh.

Table of Contents

Prologue

Welcome to the world of the Sydney Opera House, one of the most amazing and recognizable landmarks in the world! If you've ever seen pictures of Australia, you've probably noticed this fascinating building with its sail-like roofs standing proudly by the water in Sydney Harbour. But did you know that it's much more than just a pretty sight? The Sydney Opera House is a place full of incredible stories, awesome performances, and amazing architecture that captures the imagination of everyone who visits.

In this book, we're going on an exciting journey to uncover all the secrets and fun facts about this world-famous landmark. You'll learn how the Sydney Opera House was designed and built, the challenges the architects and builders faced, and how it became a symbol of creativity and culture for the entire world. We'll explore the fascinating life of Jørn Utzon, the brilliant architect behind the design, and discover how the Opera House brings together people from all over to enjoy music, plays, and so much more.

Whether you're a fan of grand concerts, cool architecture, or just curious about how this unique building came to be, there's something in here for everyone. So, get ready to dive into the stories behind one of Australia's greatest wonders—where art, music, and history come together under those shiny white sails. Let's explore the Sydney Opera House together!

Chapter 1: The Beginning of a Bold Idea

The Sydney Opera House is one of the most famous buildings in the world, and it all started with a bold idea. A long time ago, in the 1940s, people in Sydney, Australia, began thinking about building a special place where people could watch performances like concerts, plays, and operas. At that time, Sydney didn't have a large, impressive building for these events, and many people believed that the city deserved something grand and extraordinary. This idea began to grow and soon turned into a dream that would eventually shape the skyline of Sydney.

At first, many people weren't sure how to begin such a huge project. Designing a building that would stand out and be admired all over the world was no small task. They wanted something that wouldn't just be another regular building but would be unique and spectacular, something that would make people say "Wow!" when they saw it. This led the government of New South Wales, the state where Sydney is located, to announce a competition in 1956. The competition was open to architects from all over the world. The challenge was to create a design that would be unlike any other building on Earth.

Architects from many different countries started drawing their ideas and sending them in. Over 200 designs were submitted! Some of them were interesting, but none of them really captured the magic that everyone was hoping for. It seemed like finding the perfect design might be impossible—until a Danish architect named Jørn Utzon entered the competition.

Jørn Utzon's design was bold, creative, and completely different from anything anyone had ever seen before. His idea featured a series of large, curved roof structures that looked a bit like giant white sails on a ship. These sails would seem to float above the water in Sydney's harbor, creating a beautiful and eye-catching sight. His design was inspired by many things: the sails of boats in Sydney Harbor, the curves of nature, and even the wings of birds. It was something completely fresh, and it immediately stood out to the judges of the competition.

At first, some people weren't sure about Jørn Utzon's design. It was so different from the other buildings they were used to seeing. Some people thought it might be too difficult to build, while others worried that it would cost too much money. But there was something magical about his idea. It was bold and full of imagination, the kind of idea that could inspire not only the people of Sydney but also visitors from all around the world.

In 1957, after much thought, the judges decided that Jørn Utzon's design was the winner of the competition. His vision for the Opera House was exactly what they had been looking for. It was more than just a building; it was a piece of art, a structure that would make Sydney famous and would be remembered for generations to come.

But winning the competition was just the beginning of this incredible journey. Even though the idea was now in place, there was still a lot of work to do to turn the design into a real building. It wasn't going to be easy. The technology needed to build such a complex structure didn't even exist at the time! Engineers and builders would have to come up with new ways to make Utzon's vision come to life. It was a huge challenge, but everyone believed in the bold idea that had been born.

As the project moved forward, there were lots of difficulties and unexpected problems. The design of the Opera House was so advanced that it took many years to figure out how to actually build it. Sometimes, it seemed like the challenges were too big, and some people even doubted whether the Opera House would ever be finished. But despite all the obstacles, the idea remained strong. People from all over the world continued to work together, determined to bring Utzon's beautiful design to life.

Jørn Utzon's bold idea was more than just a plan for a building; it was a symbol of creativity, imagination, and the power of dreams.

It showed everyone that sometimes, the best ideas are the ones that seem impossible at first. The Sydney Opera House wouldn't be just any ordinary structure—it would be something that would inspire awe and wonder in everyone who saw it.

The beginning of this bold idea was truly a turning point for Sydney and for architecture around the world. It marked the start of a journey that would take many years to complete, but in the end, it would create one of the most iconic landmarks ever built. The Sydney Opera House is a reminder of what can happen when people dare to dream big and pursue their boldest ideas, no matter how challenging they might seem.

Chapter 2: Building the Unforgettable Structure

Building the Sydney Opera House was an extraordinary journey that took many years and presented challenges that no one had ever faced before. Turning Jørn Utzon's incredible design into a real building was far from easy. In fact, it became one of the most difficult construction projects of its time. But every part of the process was as unforgettable as the structure itself.

When the construction began in 1959, no one realized just how complex the building would be. Utzon's design was so unique that engineers had to come up with completely new methods to bring it to life. His design included those famous curved roofs, which looked like sails catching the wind. While they were beautiful and bold on paper, actually building them turned out to be a massive challenge. No one had ever created something like this before, and the technology to build such structures didn't even exist yet! This meant that everyone involved had to be incredibly inventive.

The construction was broken up into three main stages: the podium, the roof shells, and the interiors. Each stage came with its own set of problems, but none was more difficult than the roof. Let's start with the podium, the base of the building. This part of the construction began first, and it seemed fairly straightforward. The podium was a large platform that would support the entire building, and although it took a lot of time and effort to build, it didn't have the same complicated design as the roof. Still, getting everything just right was important because the whole structure had to sit perfectly on this base. It was like the foundation of a house—if the foundation wasn't strong, the rest of the building wouldn't stand. But the real challenge started when it was time to build those famous sails.

For several years, the builders and engineers couldn't figure out exactly how to create the curved shapes of the roof. Jørn Utzon's original design didn't provide detailed instructions on how the roof should be built, so they had to find a way to make the idea work. Imagine trying to make something that had never been made before, and not even knowing where to start! The engineers tried many different methods, but nothing seemed to work. Some people started to worry that the Opera House might never be finished because the roof was just too complicated. But Utzon didn't give up. He believed in his bold design and kept working on different ideas.

Finally, after years of searching for a solution, Utzon came up with a breakthrough. He realized that the roof's curves could be made from the shape of a sphere. This discovery changed everything. Instead of trying to build separate, different curves for each sail, the roof could be made using sections of the same spherical shape. This new approach made the construction of the roof possible, and the work moved forward. But it still wasn't easy. The builders had to use cranes and other special equipment to lift the heavy pieces of the roof into place. The sections were so large and heavy that they had to be carefully positioned, and even a small mistake could cause big problems. It took years to get all the pieces just right.

The roof shells were made of precast concrete, which is a type of very strong material that could hold the weight of the structure. But the builders didn't just want the roof to be strong—they wanted it to look beautiful too. This is why they covered the roof with over a million white and cream-colored ceramic tiles. These tiles weren't just there for decoration; they also helped protect the building from the harsh weather. Sydney can get very sunny, and the Opera House is right next to the water, so it needed to be able to withstand both sunlight and sea air. The tiles reflected the sunlight, making the Opera House shimmer and shine from a distance. The sight of those dazzling white sails against the blue sky and the sparkling water would become one of the most famous views in the world.

But the challenges didn't end with the roof. Building the interiors of the Opera House was just as tricky. Jørn Utzon had designed the building to have multiple performance halls, each for different types of performances, like concerts, plays, and operas. Each hall needed to have perfect acoustics, which means that the sound inside had to be just right so everyone could hear the performances clearly, no matter where they were sitting. This required a lot of planning and testing. The materials used in the walls, ceilings, and floors all had to be chosen carefully to make sure the sound was perfect.

The largest hall, called the Concert Hall, was especially difficult to design because it had to hold more than 2,000 people! It's one of the largest concert halls in the world, and making sure that everyone could hear the music clearly was a huge challenge. The shape of the room, the height of the ceiling, and even the types of seats used all had to be designed with sound in mind. But the builders and engineers worked hard, and after many adjustments, they finally created a space where the sound was just right.

There were also many other details to figure out inside the building. The Opera House was not just about the performance halls. It needed offices, rehearsal rooms, and spaces for the performers to prepare. Every part of the building had to fit perfectly together. Because of Utzon's unique design, even the smallest details had to be carefully planned. The curved walls, the large glass windows, and the wide-open spaces inside the building all had to be built in a way that matched the bold vision of the Opera House.

As the construction continued, it took longer and longer than anyone had expected. What was originally planned to take only a few years ended up taking 14 years! The delays and challenges caused the project to cost much more money than planned, and some people were frustrated. They couldn't understand why it was taking so long to finish. But those who believed in Utzon's vision knew that this was no ordinary building. The Sydney Opera House was something special, and creating something so unforgettable was bound to take time.

Unfortunately, as the project dragged on, Jørn Utzon faced more and more criticism. Some people didn't like the delays or the rising costs, and in 1966, Utzon made the difficult decision to leave the project. He never saw the Opera House finished in person. It was a sad moment in the history of the building, but his bold design remained at the heart of the project.

After Utzon left, other architects and engineers took over and completed the work. Finally, in 1973, the Sydney Opera House was ready to open its doors. Queen Elizabeth II officially opened the building on October 20, 1973, and the world was amazed. The Opera House was more than just a building—it was a symbol of creativity, imagination, and the power of bold ideas. The people of Sydney were proud of their new landmark, and it quickly became famous all around the globe.

Even though the construction of the Sydney Opera House was filled with difficulties, the final result was nothing short of spectacular. The unforgettable structure stands as a testament to the hard work, determination, and vision of everyone who believed in Jørn Utzon's design. It's a reminder that sometimes, the most challenging projects are the ones that leave the greatest legacy. Today, millions of people visit the Sydney Opera House every year, and its unique shape and incredible history continue to inspire people all over the world.

Chapter 3: The Story of Architect Jørn Utzon

The story of Jørn Utzon, the architect behind the Sydney Opera House, is a fascinating tale of creativity, vision, perseverance, and challenges. Born on April 9, 1918, in Copenhagen, Denmark, Jørn Utzon grew up in a family that encouraged creativity and a deep connection to the arts. His father, Aage Utzon, was a naval engineer, and from a young age, Jørn was exposed to the world of design, construction, and innovation. Watching his father work on ships, young Jørn developed an early love for architecture and design, fascinated by how different elements of a structure could come together to create something functional and beautiful.

As he grew older, Jørn Utzon pursued his passion for architecture and attended the Royal Danish Academy of Fine Arts in Copenhagen. There, he was mentored by some of the most respected architects of the time, which helped him refine his ideas and develop a bold, modern style. Utzon wasn't interested in copying old architectural traditions. He was inspired by nature and wanted to create buildings that reflected the organic shapes and patterns found in the world around him. He was also fascinated by how light, space, and movement could be used to enhance a building's design. This creative approach to architecture would eventually lead him to develop the iconic design of the Sydney Opera House.

Before the Opera House, Jørn Utzon was still relatively unknown in the world of architecture. He had worked on various projects in Denmark and a few in other parts of Europe, but he hadn't yet had the opportunity to create something truly groundbreaking. That changed in 1956, when a global competition was announced to design a new opera house for Sydney, Australia. The competition drew over 200 entries from architects all around the world, and the challenge was clear: create a building that was not only functional but also iconic, a structure that would become a symbol of Sydney and of Australia as a whole.

When Jørn Utzon heard about the competition, he saw it as the perfect opportunity to push the boundaries of architecture. He wanted to create something that had never been seen before, a building that would capture the imagination of people everywhere. Inspired by the natural beauty of Sydney's harbor, as well as his lifelong fascination with the curves and shapes found in nature, Utzon began sketching designs for what would eventually become the Sydney Opera House. He imagined a series of white, sail-like structures that would rise above the harbor, reflecting the waves of the water and the sails of the ships that passed by. It was a bold idea, unlike anything anyone had ever seen, and it was risky too. The design seemed almost impossible to build, but Utzon believed in his vision.

When the judges of the competition first saw Utzon's design, they were immediately struck by its originality and beauty. One of the most famous architects of the time, Eero Saarinen, who was on the judging panel, reportedly pulled Utzon's design from a pile of rejected entries, exclaiming, "This is the winner." And he was right. In 1957, Jørn Utzon's design was chosen as the winning entry, and he was given the task of turning his vision into a reality. It was a dream come true for Utzon, but it was also the beginning of one of the most challenging periods of his life.

Although Jørn Utzon had won the competition, actually building the Opera House proved to be incredibly difficult. His design was so complex that the engineers and builders had no idea how to make it work. The roof, in particular, was a huge challenge. It was made up of large, curved shells, but at the time, there was no technology that could easily create such shapes. For years, Utzon worked closely with engineers, trying to figure out how to construct the roof in a way that would match his vision. There were many setbacks, and some people began to doubt whether the project would ever be completed.

During this time, Jørn Utzon also faced increasing pressure from the government and other officials in Sydney. The Opera House project was taking longer than expected, and the costs were rising. Originally, the building was supposed to take just a few years to complete, but as the construction dragged on and on, it became clear that it would take much longer. Many people blamed Utzon for the delays, even though the challenges they faced were due to the revolutionary nature of his design. As the years passed, the cost of the project continued to grow, and politicians began to criticize Utzon's leadership.

Despite these difficulties, Utzon never gave up on his dream. He continued to work on the design, believing that once the building was complete, it would be a masterpiece. He also continued to innovate, coming up with new ideas and solutions to solve the problems that arose during construction. One of his greatest breakthroughs came when he realized that the curved roof shells could be made from sections of a single sphere. This discovery helped simplify the construction process and allowed the builders to finally move forward with the roof.

Unfortunately, even though Utzon had made great progress, his struggles with the government and the construction team continued. In 1966, after nearly a decade of working on the project, the pressure became too much, and Jørn Utzon made the heartbreaking decision to resign from the project. He left Australia and returned to Denmark, never seeing the Opera House completed in person. It was a devastating blow for Utzon, who had poured so much of his heart and soul into the design. He had dreamed of seeing the Opera House finished, but it seemed that dream would never come true.

After Utzon's resignation, other architects were brought in to complete the building. Although they followed many of Utzon's original plans, some changes were made, particularly to the interior of the building. These changes meant that the finished Opera House was not exactly as Utzon had envisioned it, but his iconic design still remained the heart and soul of the building. Finally, in 1973, the Sydney Opera House was completed, and it was officially opened by Queen Elizabeth II. The world was amazed by the beauty and grandeur of the building, and it quickly became a symbol of Australia and an icon of modern architecture.

Even though Jørn Utzon wasn't there to see the opening of the Opera House, his legacy lived on in the building. People from all over the world admired his bold vision, and over time, his role in creating the Opera House was celebrated more and more. In 2003, many years after the Opera House was completed, Jørn Utzon was awarded the prestigious Pritzker Architecture Prize, the highest honor an architect can receive. In their statement, the jury praised Utzon for his "masterpiece" and for creating one of the most iconic buildings in the world. Although Utzon was modest and rarely sought attention, this recognition meant a great deal to him. It was a reminder that, despite all the challenges and setbacks he had faced, his vision had made a lasting impact on the world.

In the later years of his life, Jørn Utzon was invited to collaborate on updates and renovations to the Sydney Opera House, even though he never returned to Australia. His son, Jan Utzon, also an architect, played a key role in helping to carry on his father's vision. Together, they worked on plans to restore and enhance some of the parts of the Opera House that had been changed after Utzon left the project. This allowed Jørn Utzon to have a lasting influence on the building, even after all those years.

Jørn Utzon passed away in 2008 at the age of 90, but his legacy continues to inspire architects, artists, and dreamers around the world. The Sydney Opera House stands as a testament to his genius, his creativity, and his ability to think outside the box. It's a reminder that sometimes, the most groundbreaking ideas come from those who dare to dream big and take risks. Utzon's story shows that even when the path is difficult and full of obstacles, staying true to your vision can lead to something truly extraordinary.

Today, millions of people visit the Sydney Opera House every year, and each time they see its stunning white sails rising above the harbor, they are witnessing the result of Jørn Utzon's bold idea. His design has become a symbol of Australia and one of the most famous buildings in the world. The story of Jørn Utzon and the Sydney Opera House reminds us that architecture isn't just about building structures—it's about creating something that captures the imagination and leaves a lasting legacy for generations to come.

Chapter 4: How the Sydney Opera House Got Its Shape

The Sydney Opera House is one of the most recognizable buildings in the world, and one of the things that makes it so famous is its incredible shape. The design of the Opera House is truly unique—its roof looks like giant white sails or seashells, almost as if a group of sailboats are gliding on Sydney's harbor or a collection of shells has been carefully arranged by the water. But how did the Sydney Opera House get its shape? It all started with a vision from the architect Jørn Utzon, who wanted to create something bold, different, and connected to nature. This is the story of how the Opera House's iconic shape came to be.

When Jørn Utzon entered the design competition to create the Sydney Opera House in 1956, he knew that he wanted to design something that would stand out from any other building in the world. The location of the building, on Bennelong Point in Sydney, was right by the harbor, and Utzon was inspired by the natural beauty of the site. He felt that the building should not only fit into its surroundings but also reflect the spirit of Sydney, a city known for its connection to the water and its bustling harbor filled with sailboats. He wanted to design a building that looked like it belonged there, as if it was part of the landscape and the sea.

Utzon's original idea for the Opera House was to make the roof look like a series of sails, billowing in the wind as they moved across the water. This idea came to him as he sketched different concepts, trying to capture the essence of movement and lightness. He didn't want the building to have a flat, boxy design like many other buildings at the time. Instead, he wanted it to be dynamic, with a sense of motion and energy, just like the waves in the harbor or the sails of a boat. He also wanted the design to be open and inviting, so that people would feel like they were stepping into something exciting and different when they approached the building.

The curved shapes of the roof were also influenced by Utzon's love for organic forms found in nature. He had traveled to many parts of the world and had been inspired by everything from the rounded roofs of traditional Japanese temples to the smooth curves of the shells he saw on the beaches. He admired the way that nature created beautiful, functional shapes without straight lines or sharp edges, and he wanted to bring some of that natural beauty into his design for the Opera House. Utzon believed that architecture should mimic the shapes and forms of the natural world, and his design for the Opera House was a way to bring that belief to life.

Once Utzon had the idea of making the roof look like sails, the next challenge was figuring out how to actually build those shapes. This was not an easy task. In fact, when Utzon first presented his design, many engineers and builders were confused. They had never seen a roof design like this before, and they weren't sure how they would be able to construct it. The curved shells that Utzon wanted to create were incredibly complex, and at first, no one could figure out how to make them strong enough to hold up the roof while still keeping the graceful, flowing shape that Utzon had in mind.

For years, Utzon and his team worked on solving this problem. One of the biggest challenges was the fact that the shapes were so unusual. Traditional roofs were made of flat, straight pieces that were much easier to construct. But Utzon's design didn't have any straight lines—it was all about curves and arcs, which meant that the builders had to come up with entirely new ways of constructing the roof. The original idea was to make the roof from individual curved pieces, each one built separately and then fitted together like a giant puzzle. But after a lot of trial and error, it became clear that this method wouldn't work. The pieces were too difficult to create, and they wouldn't fit together in the way that Utzon had imagined.

In the early stages of construction, some people began to doubt whether the project would ever be completed. The builders had started working on the foundation of the Opera House, but they still didn't know how they would be able to build the roof. As time went on, the pressure to find a solution grew stronger, and Utzon and his team had to think creatively to come up with a new approach. That's when Utzon had a breakthrough idea that would change everything. He realized that instead of trying to build each curved shell individually, he could create all the shapes from sections of a single sphere. This idea, called the "spherical solution," made it possible to construct the complex shapes of the roof in a much simpler and more efficient way.

The spherical solution was a turning point in the construction of the Opera House. By using segments of a sphere, Utzon's team could build each shell from smaller, more manageable pieces, which could then be assembled to form the larger curves of the roof. This made the construction process much easier and allowed the builders to move forward with creating the distinctive shape of the Opera House. The shells were made from precast concrete panels, which were molded into the perfect shape before being lifted into place. Each shell was made up of several smaller pieces, but when they were assembled, they formed the smooth, flowing curves that Utzon had imagined in his original design.

The shapes of the roof aren't just beautiful to look at—they also serve an important purpose in making the building functional. The tall, curved shells help create large, open spaces inside the Opera House, where sound can move freely and fill the room during performances. This was another one of Utzon's goals: to design a building where people could experience music, theater, and opera in a space that felt grand and open. The height and shape of the shells help the sound travel, creating a rich, immersive experience for everyone inside.

While the roof of the Opera House is its most famous feature, the design of the entire building is carefully crafted to reflect the shapes and forms found in nature. The base of the Opera House is designed to look like a series of large platforms, almost like terraces rising out of the harbor. These terraces are made of large, rectangular stones, which contrast with the smooth, rounded shapes of the roof above. This contrast between the solid, angular base and the light, flowing roof is one of the things that makes the building so striking. It feels like the roof is floating above the base, almost as if it's about to take off into the sky.

The roof's white color was also carefully chosen to enhance the overall effect of the design. Utzon wanted the roof to reflect the light and colors of the harbor, so he chose to cover the shells with thousands of white ceramic tiles. These tiles catch the sunlight during the day, making the Opera House shine brightly against the blue sky and the water. At night, the tiles reflect the lights of the city, giving the building a magical glow that can be seen from miles away. The color and texture of the roof help the Opera House blend into its surroundings, while still making it stand out as a bold, iconic structure.

Another fascinating aspect of the roof's design is how it changes depending on where you're standing. From up close, the curved shells look enormous, towering above the people walking around the building. But from farther away, the roof seems to shrink and become part of the landscape, almost as if it's blending into the horizon. The different angles and perspectives create a sense of movement, making the building feel alive, as if it's constantly shifting and changing with the light and the weather. This dynamic quality is one of the reasons why the Sydney Opera House is so beloved—it feels like a living, breathing part of the city, always interacting with its environment.

Although the shape of the Sydney Opera House was incredibly challenging to create, it has become one of the most admired designs in the world. Jørn Utzon's vision for a building that reflected the natural beauty of Sydney's harbor has been realized in a way that continues to inspire people from all over the globe. The curved shells of the roof have become a symbol of Sydney, and they represent not only the creativity and innovation of Jørn Utzon but also the idea that architecture can be both functional and artistic. The shape of the Sydney Opera House is more than just a design—it's a work of art that captures the imagination and leaves a lasting impression on everyone who sees it.

Today, the Sydney Opera House is considered one of the greatest architectural achievements of the 20th century. Its shape, inspired by nature and brought to life through innovative engineering, has made it an enduring symbol of Australia and a global icon. The story of how the Sydney Opera House got its shape is a reminder of the power of creativity, determination, and the ability to think outside the box. It shows that even the most difficult challenges can be overcome with bold ideas and a willingness to explore new possibilities.

Chapter 5: A Home for Music, Dance, and Drama

The Sydney Opera House is not just a building with a striking design; it's a home for music, dance, drama, and countless other forms of artistic expression. Over the years, it has become one of the most important cultural centers in the world. Inside its walls, artists from all over the globe gather to perform, create, and share their talents with audiences who come from near and far to experience the magic of live performances. But what makes the Sydney Opera House such a special place for music, dance, and drama? To understand that, we need to dive deep into what happens within this iconic structure and how it has been built to celebrate the arts in the most extraordinary way.

When Jørn Utzon first envisioned the Sydney Opera House, he didn't just want to create an impressive building; he wanted to design a space where the arts could thrive. From the very beginning, it was intended to be a place where people could come together to experience live performances in a setting that was as inspiring as the performances themselves. The idea was to create a building that would uplift both the performers and the audience, making every visit to the Opera House a memorable occasion. Today, that vision has come to life in more ways than Utzon could have imagined.

One of the most important things about the Sydney Opera House is that it was designed to host a wide variety of performances. From grand operas and orchestral concerts to contemporary dance, theater, and even stand-up comedy, the Opera House has become a stage for all forms of artistic expression. Its diverse program means that there's something for everyone—whether you love classical music, ballet, drama, or the latest in modern entertainment. This flexibility was built into the design of the building, with multiple performance halls that can each be adapted for different types of shows.

The largest performance space in the Sydney Opera House is the Concert Hall. This massive auditorium can hold over 2,000 people, making it one of the largest concert halls in the world. The Concert Hall is primarily used for music performances, especially orchestral and classical concerts, but it can also be adapted for other types of shows. When you step into the Concert Hall, you're immediately struck by its grandeur. The towering ceilings, the elegant wood paneling, and the sense of space all come together to create an atmosphere that feels almost sacred, like you're entering a special place where something incredible is about to happen.

But it's not just about how the Concert Hall looks—it's also about how it sounds. The acoustics of the hall have been carefully designed to ensure that every note played on stage is heard perfectly by the audience, no matter where they are sitting. The shape of the hall, the materials used in its construction, and even the placement of the seats have all been planned to create the best possible sound experience. Musicians who perform in the Concert Hall often say that it's one of the best places in the world to play because the sound is so clear and rich. For audiences, this means that they can hear every detail of the music, from the softest notes of a violin to the thunderous boom of a drum.

Another important performance space within the Sydney Opera House is the Joan Sutherland Theatre, named after one of Australia's most famous opera singers. This theater is primarily used for opera and ballet performances, making it the perfect home for productions that combine music, singing, and dance. Like the Concert Hall, the Joan Sutherland Theatre has been designed with both performers and audiences in mind. The stage is large enough to accommodate elaborate sets, dancers, and full orchestras, while the seating is arranged to give everyone a clear view of the action. Whether you're watching a grand opera or a graceful ballet, the Joan Sutherland Theatre offers an intimate experience that brings the magic of live performance to life.

The Opera House also has smaller theaters, including the Drama Theatre and the Playhouse, which are ideal for more intimate performances. These spaces are often used for plays, one-person shows, experimental theater, and smaller musical performances. The smaller size of these theaters allows for a closer connection between the performers and the audience, creating a sense of intimacy that is perfect for dramatic works and personal storytelling. Whether you're watching a classic Shakespeare play or a modern drama, the smaller theaters in the Sydney Opera House offer a unique experience where every gesture, word, and movement feels immediate and personal.

One of the most exciting things about the Sydney Opera House is that it's not just a place for traditional performances—it also embraces the new and the experimental. Over the years, the Opera House has welcomed everything from cutting-edge contemporary dance troupes to electronic music festivals, spoken word events, and multimedia art installations. This openness to new forms of expression has made the Sydney Opera House a hub for creative innovation. Artists from all over the world come to the Opera House to push the boundaries of their craft, experimenting with new technologies, ideas, and styles to create performances that challenge and inspire.

The Opera House's role as a home for the arts extends beyond the performances that happen on its stages. It also plays a crucial role in nurturing new talent and giving young and emerging artists a platform to showcase their work. Through programs like the Sydney Opera House Trust's creative development initiatives, the building has become a place where young musicians, actors, dancers, and playwrights can explore their creativity and grow as artists. These programs provide opportunities for artists to work with mentors, collaborate with other performers, and develop their skills in a supportive environment. For many artists, performing at the Sydney Opera House is a dream come true and a major milestone in their careers.

In addition to its role as a home for performers, the Sydney Opera House is also a gathering place for audiences. People from all walks of life come to the Opera House to experience the magic of live performance. Whether they're locals from Sydney or tourists visiting from other countries, audiences are drawn to the Opera House not just for the performances, but for the sense of community that it fosters. When you attend a performance at the Opera House, you're sharing the experience with hundreds or even thousands of other people, all coming together to be moved, entertained, and inspired. This sense of shared experience is one of the most powerful things about live performance, and the Sydney Opera House provides the perfect setting for it.

One of the things that makes the Opera House so special is that it's not just a place where you go to watch a performance—it's also a place to explore, discover, and learn. The Opera House offers a wide range of educational programs for children, families, and schools, giving young people the chance to learn about music, theater, dance, and the arts in a hands-on way. These programs include workshops, backstage tours, and special performances designed for kids. By offering these opportunities, the Sydney Opera House is helping to inspire the next generation of artists and audiences, encouraging young people to develop a love for the arts that will last a lifetime.

Another important aspect of the Sydney Opera House's role as a home for the arts is its connection to the wider world. The Opera House regularly hosts international performers and companies, bringing the best of global culture to Sydney's shores. Whether it's a world-famous orchestra, a renowned dance company, or a celebrated theater troupe, the Opera House attracts top talent from all over the globe. This international exchange enriches Sydney's cultural scene and gives audiences the chance to experience performances from different cultures and traditions. At the same time, the Opera House also plays a key role in promoting Australian talent on the world stage, helping local artists gain recognition and appreciation beyond Australia's borders.

The Sydney Opera House is more than just a place to watch performances—it's a symbol of the power of the arts to bring people together. Through its diverse range of performances, educational programs, and commitment to innovation, the Opera House has become a beacon of creativity and culture. It's a place where music, dance, and drama are celebrated in all their forms, from the classical to the cutting-edge. For performers, it's a stage where dreams come true, and for audiences, it's a place where they can be transported to new worlds through the magic of live performance.

Perhaps one of the most amazing things about the Sydney Opera House is how it continues to evolve and grow. Even though it was completed decades ago, the Opera House remains as relevant and vibrant as ever. It constantly adapts to the changing world of the arts, embracing new technologies, new forms of expression, and new ways of engaging with audiences. In this way, the Sydney Opera House is not just a home for music, dance, and drama—it's a living, breathing part of the cultural fabric of Australia and the world. Its story is far from over, and as long as there are artists and audiences who believe in the power of the arts, the Sydney Opera House will continue to inspire and amaze for generations to come.

Chapter 6: Secrets of the Opera House Shells

The Sydney Opera House is known all around the world for its unique and breathtaking design, and the most famous part of that design is the shells that seem to float above the building. These white, sail-like shapes give the Opera House its iconic look, making it instantly recognizable and one of the most photographed buildings on the planet. But there's so much more to these shells than meets the eye. They aren't just there to look beautiful; they're a marvel of architecture, engineering, and creativity. Let's explore the secrets of these incredible structures, the story behind them, and how they were built to become the defining feature of this world-famous landmark.

When Jørn Utzon first imagined the design of the Sydney Opera House, he wanted the building to reflect the beauty of Sydney Harbour. He was inspired by the natural shapes around him—the sails of boats gliding across the water, the curve of seashells found on the beach, and even the rounded forms of clouds in the sky. These elements of nature became the foundation for his vision of the Opera House, and that's how the idea of creating the distinctive shells came to be. However, turning these flowing, organic shapes into a real, functioning building was no easy task. In fact, the shells posed one of the biggest challenges in the entire construction process.

When the design was first presented, many people were amazed by how bold and artistic it looked. But behind the scenes, engineers and builders were scratching their heads, trying to figure out how to bring Utzon's vision to life. The challenge wasn't just about making the shells look like sails or waves; it was about creating a structure that could actually stand up, be safe, and function as a building. Early on, the construction team realized that the shells couldn't just be built in the usual way. They needed to be strong enough to support their own weight, provide shelter for the performance halls below, and still maintain their elegant, curved shape.

At first, the engineers tried different methods to create the shells, but nothing seemed to work. They experimented with a range of ideas, from different materials to construction techniques, but all of their attempts either looked wrong or weren't structurally sound. It seemed like the shells would be impossible to build—until Jørn Utzon had a breakthrough idea. He realized that the answer lay in geometry, specifically in the shape of a sphere.

Utzon's big breakthrough came when he decided that all the shells should be parts of the same sphere. Imagine a large, round ball, and then imagine cutting out pieces of that ball to create different curved shapes. By doing this, Utzon was able to create shells that all had a uniform, mathematical structure, making them much easier to build. This idea of using spherical geometry solved the puzzle and allowed the construction team to create the shells in a way that was both beautiful and structurally sound.

Once the design of the shells was finalized, the next challenge was building them. The shells are made up of hundreds of concrete panels that were prefabricated—meaning they were built off-site and then transported to the construction site to be assembled. Each panel was carefully shaped to fit perfectly with the others, forming the smooth, curved surfaces of the shells. This method of construction was groundbreaking at the time, and it allowed the builders to create the complex shapes that make the Opera House so unique.

But the shells aren't just about their outer appearance. Inside, they serve an important purpose, too. The shells cover the performance halls below, creating a protective roof that allows sound to travel properly and keeps the spaces below dry and comfortable, even in the worst weather. The way the shells are arranged also helps to bring natural light into the building. Light filters through the gaps between the shells, creating a soft, glowing effect inside the Opera House, which adds to the sense of wonder that visitors feel when they enter the building.

The materials used to build the shells are just as fascinating as their design. The outer surface of the shells is covered with over one million tiles. These tiles are small, white, and glossy, giving the shells their iconic shimmering appearance. From a distance, the tiles make the shells look smooth and clean, but when you get up close, you can see that they have a subtle texture. The tiles are not just there for decoration, though—they were chosen specifically because they reflect sunlight beautifully while also helping to keep the building cool. In the hot Australian sun, the white tiles reflect heat, which keeps the interior of the Opera House from getting too warm.

Another secret of the Opera House shells is their ability to withstand the elements. Sydney is a city that experiences a wide range of weather conditions, from blazing hot summers to heavy rains and strong winds. The shells were designed to handle all of this without any problems. The shape of the shells allows rainwater to run off easily, preventing water from pooling on the roof. At the same time, the strong, curved structure of the shells helps them to resist the force of the wind, even during storms. Over the decades, the shells have proven to be incredibly durable, standing up to the test of time and the harsh elements of the Australian climate.

Inside the shells, the spaces are just as impressive as the outside. When you step into the Sydney Opera House, you're surrounded by towering, curved walls that create a sense of grandeur and elegance. The way the shells curve overhead makes the spaces inside feel almost like a cathedral, with high, soaring ceilings that seem to stretch up to the sky. This sense of openness and space is one of the things that makes the Opera House so special. The architecture itself feels like a work of art, making every visit feel like a magical experience.

One of the most interesting things about the shells is how they change throughout the day and night. During the day, the shells gleam in the sunlight, casting soft shadows on the building and reflecting the bright blue of the sky. At sunset, the colors of the shells shift, taking on a warm, golden glow as the sun dips below the horizon. And at night, the shells come alive with light, as they are often illuminated by special lighting displays that change their color and appearance. These lighting displays can be used to celebrate special occasions, support important causes, or simply showcase the beauty of the building.

Over the years, the Sydney Opera House shells have become a symbol of Sydney itself. They represent creativity, innovation, and the spirit of adventure that the city is known for. People from all over the world recognize the shells as a symbol of Australia's cultural identity, and they have become one of the most iconic landmarks on the planet. When people think of Sydney, they often think of the Opera House and its striking shells rising above the harbor.

The story of the Opera House shells is a story of persistence, creativity, and vision. What started as a bold idea that many thought was impossible became one of the greatest architectural achievements of the 20th century. Jørn Utzon's vision for a building that reflected the natural beauty of Sydney Harbour became a reality, thanks to the hard work and dedication of the engineers, builders, and artists who brought his design to life. Today, the shells stand as a testament to the power of imagination and the incredible things that can happen when people work together to turn a dream into reality.

As visitors walk around the Opera House, they can marvel at the beauty and complexity of the shells, knowing that they are not just a beautiful design but also a triumph of engineering and artistic vision. These shells hold many secrets—secrets of geometry, construction, and innovation—that make them more than just a roof over a building. They are a masterpiece, a symbol of human creativity, and an enduring part of Sydney's skyline. For generations to come, people will continue to be inspired by the Sydney Opera House shells, and the magic they bring to the heart of Sydney Harbour.

Chapter 7: The Grand Opening Celebration

The grand opening of the Sydney Opera House was a moment that the people of Australia, and the world, would never forget. After years of construction, challenges, and anticipation, this magnificent building, with its shimmering white shells, was finally ready to be unveiled to the public. It was October 20, 1973, a day filled with excitement, pride, and joy as people gathered to witness the grand celebration. This wasn't just any ordinary event; it was a historic moment marking the completion of one of the most ambitious architectural projects of the century. The opening of the Sydney Opera House symbolized a new chapter in Australia's cultural story, and the celebrations that followed were as grand and spectacular as the building itself.

Leading up to the grand opening, there was a buzz of anticipation throughout Sydney. People had been watching the progress of the Opera House for years, and the unique design had captured the imagination of people around the world. When the big day finally arrived, thousands of people flocked to Sydney Harbour to witness the celebrations firsthand. Boats filled the harbor, people lined the shores, and a sense of excitement filled the air as everyone waited to see what was in store.

One of the highlights of the grand opening was the attendance of Queen Elizabeth II. The Queen's presence made the occasion even more special, as she was there to officially declare the Sydney Opera House open. Dressed in elegant attire, Queen Elizabeth stood on the steps of the Opera House, surrounded by dignitaries and government officials, as the world watched. It was a moment of great pride for Australia, as the Queen's involvement in the event signaled the international significance of the Opera House. The building wasn't just a symbol of Sydney or Australia—it had become a global icon.

The grand opening ceremony was full of pomp and pageantry, with a sense of spectacle that matched the grandeur of the Opera House itself. The event started with a traditional Aboriginal welcome, paying homage to the original custodians of the land on which the Opera House stands. This was an important part of the celebration, recognizing the deep cultural history of the area and honoring the Gadigal people of the Eora Nation. The blending of ancient traditions with modern celebrations highlighted the rich cultural diversity of Australia.

As part of the ceremony, there were performances from some of Australia's most talented artists and musicians. The Sydney Symphony Orchestra played majestic music that filled the air and echoed across the harbor. It was fitting that music played such a central role in the opening, as the Sydney Opera House was designed to be a home for the arts, especially music, dance, and drama. The orchestra's performance set the tone for what the Opera House would become—a place where the finest performances from around the world would take place.

After the orchestral performance, there were other musical acts, dancers, and entertainers who took to the stage, showcasing the talent and creativity of Australia's performing arts community. Each performance was a celebration of the Opera House's purpose: to be a space where artists could come together to create something magical. The diverse range of performances reflected the Opera House's future as a world-class venue for all kinds of artistic expression, from classical music to contemporary dance, opera to theater, and everything in between.

In addition to the musical performances, there were speeches from government leaders and dignitaries, who spoke about the significance of the Opera House and the long journey it took to bring the building to life. They spoke of Jørn Utzon's visionary design, the hard work of the construction teams, and the challenges that had been overcome to complete the project. The speeches were filled with pride and emotion, as everyone involved in the project understood that this was more than just a building—it was a masterpiece that would stand as a symbol of human achievement for generations to come.

One of the most memorable moments of the grand opening was when Queen Elizabeth officially declared the Sydney Opera House open. With the harbor glistening behind her, she pulled a cord, which unfurled a giant banner across the front of the Opera House. The banner read "Sydney Opera House Open," and as it was revealed, the crowd erupted into cheers and applause. It was a moment of pure joy and celebration, as people realized that this dream had finally become a reality.

As the opening ceremony continued, there was a spectacular fireworks display that lit up the night sky over Sydney Harbour. The Opera House, with its gleaming white shells, was illuminated by the colorful bursts of light, creating a breathtaking scene. The fireworks were a fitting tribute to the achievement of building such an extraordinary structure. They filled the sky with dazzling colors, lighting up the sails of the Opera House and reflecting off the waters of the harbor. It was a sight that left everyone in awe and perfectly captured the grandeur of the occasion.

The fireworks weren't just a celebration of the Opera House itself—they were also a celebration of the people who had worked so hard to make it happen. From Jørn Utzon's original design to the engineers who solved the many technical challenges, to the construction workers who toiled for years, the opening of the Sydney Opera House was a testament to their dedication and perseverance. The fireworks symbolized the culmination of their efforts and the bright future that lay ahead for the Opera House as a beacon of culture and creativity.

As the grand opening celebrations continued into the night, there were parties and festivities throughout the city. The opening of the Sydney Opera House was more than just a one-day event—it was a moment that united the entire city of Sydney, and indeed the entire country. People from all walks of life joined in the celebrations, whether they were attending the official ceremony or watching it on television. The Opera House became a symbol of Australian pride and a representation of the nation's cultural aspirations.

The grand opening of the Sydney Opera House also had a significant impact on the world stage. News outlets from around the globe covered the event, and the images of the Opera House's stunning architecture and vibrant celebrations were broadcast to millions of viewers. The Opera House quickly became an international icon, with people from all over the world eager to visit and see this architectural wonder for themselves. The grand opening cemented the Sydney Opera House's status as one of the most famous and admired buildings in the world.

In the days and weeks following the grand opening, the Opera House continued to host special performances and events, each one further showcasing the building's incredible design and its role as a cultural hub. From opera and ballet to theater and orchestral concerts, the Opera House's stages were filled with performances that delighted audiences and demonstrated the versatility of the venue. The acoustics, designed to enhance the sound of every performance, proved to be among the best in the world, making the Sydney Opera House a dream destination for artists and performers.

The grand opening celebrations of the Sydney Opera House marked the beginning of a new era for Sydney and for Australia. It wasn't just about the completion of a building; it was about the realization of a vision that had captured the hearts and minds of people across the country and the world. The Opera House became a symbol of what could be achieved through creativity, hard work, and a commitment to excellence. It stood as a reminder that even the most ambitious dreams can become reality with determination and ingenuity.

To this day, the memory of the grand opening lives on in the hearts of those who were there to witness it and in the stories passed down to new generations. The Sydney Opera House continues to be a source of pride for Australians and a destination for millions of visitors who come to admire its beauty and experience its magic. The grand opening was not just a one-time event, but the beginning of a legacy that will last for centuries, as the Sydney Opera House continues to inspire and captivate people from all corners of the globe.

Chapter 8: Life on the Sydney Harbour

Life on Sydney Harbour is an ever-changing, vibrant blend of natural beauty, human activity, and rich history that unfolds along the shores and waters of one of the most iconic harbors in the world. Nestled within the heart of Sydney, the harbor is like the city's beating heart, constantly buzzing with life. Whether it's the gentle lapping of waves against the shore, the sight of boats gliding across the water, or the colorful ferries transporting people from one side to the other, the harbor is alive with movement and energy, a place where locals and visitors come to soak up the essence of Sydney.

From the earliest times, long before the first Europeans arrived, Sydney Harbour was already full of life. The Aboriginal people of the Eora Nation, including the Gadigal, Cammeraygal, and Wangal clans, called this place home for thousands of years. The waters of the harbor were their source of food, culture, and connection to the land. They fished in the waters, gathered shellfish along the shore, and built their communities around the natural bounty that the harbor provided. The harbor was more than just a place to live—it was a sacred and spiritual part of their culture, and the people lived in harmony with the natural environment, respecting the land and the sea as important parts of their identity.

As Sydney grew from a small colony into a bustling city, the harbor became even more central to life in the area. The early settlers relied on the harbor for trade, transportation, and food, much like the Aboriginal people before them. Boats carried goods and people between different parts of the colony, and the harbor became a gateway to the rest of the world. The ships that sailed into Sydney Harbour brought supplies from faraway places, and in return, they took goods back to other parts of the globe. The hustle and bustle of the harbor were signs of a city that was growing and thriving, with the harbor as its lifeline to the wider world.

Over time, Sydney Harbour evolved into a place not just for work but also for leisure. Today, the harbor is one of the most beloved spots in the city, a place where people come to relax, enjoy nature, and take in the stunning views. One of the most beautiful sights on the harbor is the Sydney Opera House, with its shimmering white sails standing out against the blue water. People from all over the world come to Sydney to visit the Opera House, and many enjoy taking a ferry ride or boat cruise to see it from the water. The sight of the Opera House and the nearby Sydney Harbour Bridge, with boats sailing underneath, is one of the most famous images of Australia.

There is always something happening on Sydney Harbour. The ferries that travel back and forth across the water are a familiar sight, with their bright colors and cheerful passengers. Many Sydneysiders use the ferries as a regular part of their daily commute, traveling between their homes in suburbs like Manly or Balmain and the central business district. For tourists, riding a ferry is one of the best ways to see the harbor. From the deck of a ferry, you can take in the wide expanse of the water, the green parks and gardens that line the shore, and the towering buildings of the city skyline in the distance. It's a peaceful and picturesque way to experience the harbor, with the wind in your hair and the salty sea breeze on your face.

In addition to the ferries, Sydney Harbour is full of boats of all kinds. Sailboats, yachts, speedboats, and even giant cruise ships make their way through the harbor every day. On a sunny afternoon, you can see colorful sails dotting the horizon as people set out on their boats to enjoy the water. Some people love to sail or fish in the harbor, while others enjoy kayaking or paddleboarding along the quieter coves and inlets. For those who don't own a boat, there are plenty of boat tours and harbor cruises that take people around the harbor, showing off all its famous landmarks and hidden gems.

The waters of the harbor are teeming with life, not just human activity but also a rich array of marine creatures. Beneath the surface, the harbor is home to a diverse ecosystem of fish, crustaceans, and other sea life. Fishermen often cast their lines into the water from boats or from the shore, hoping to catch species like bream, flathead, or kingfish. In the more secluded areas of the harbor, you might even spot dolphins swimming gracefully through the water or see pelicans gliding over the surface, searching for their next meal. The harbor's marine environment is carefully protected, and there are ongoing efforts to keep the water clean and ensure that the animals who live there can thrive.

The shores of Sydney Harbour are lined with parks, beaches, and walking paths, offering plenty of places for people to enjoy the natural beauty of the area. One of the most popular spots is the Royal Botanic Garden, which stretches along the harbor's edge, providing stunning views of the water and the city skyline. People come to the gardens to picnic, relax, and take in the scenery. There are also numerous beaches scattered around the harbor, such as Balmoral Beach and Camp Cove, where families and friends gather to swim, play, and soak up the sun. The combination of city life and nature is one of the things that makes Sydney Harbour so special—you can be in the heart of a major metropolis one minute and surrounded by serene natural beauty the next.

Life on Sydney Harbour is also marked by a number of special events and festivals that bring people together to celebrate. One of the most famous is the Sydney New Year's Eve fireworks, which light up the sky over the harbor every year. Hundreds of thousands of people gather along the shores and on boats to watch the dazzling display, which is broadcast to millions of viewers around the world. The fireworks over the Sydney Harbour Bridge are a spectacular way to ring in the new year, and the event is one of the most anticipated celebrations in the city.

Another beloved event is the Sydney to Hobart Yacht Race, which begins on Boxing Day each year. The race starts in Sydney Harbour, with hundreds of yachts sailing out into the open ocean as thousands of spectators cheer them on from the shore. The sight of the sleek yachts cutting through the water is a thrilling experience, and the race has become one of the most prestigious and challenging sailing competitions in the world.

Sydney Harbour is also home to important cultural institutions like the Museum of Contemporary Art, which overlooks the water, and the Australian National Maritime Museum, which tells the story of Australia's rich maritime history. The museum features historic ships and exhibits that explore the connection between Australia and the sea, from the early Indigenous canoes to the ships that brought the first European settlers to the country. These cultural landmarks add another layer of depth to life on the harbor, reminding visitors and locals alike of the important role the harbor has played throughout Sydney's history.

As day turns to night, the harbor takes on a new kind of beauty. The city lights reflect off the water, and the Opera House and the Harbour Bridge are illuminated, creating a magical scene. Restaurants and cafes along the waterfront fill with people enjoying a meal with a view, while others take evening walks along the promenades, savoring the cool night air. Even after the sun sets, the harbor continues to pulse with life, as boats pass by in the distance and the sounds of the city blend with the gentle rhythm of the waves.

In every season, life on Sydney Harbour offers something special. In the summer, the water is alive with activity as people swim, sail, and enjoy the warm weather. In the cooler months, the harbor takes on a more tranquil feel, but it remains just as beautiful, with misty mornings and calm waters. Whether it's the lively festivals, the quiet moments of reflection, or the everyday hustle and bustle, Sydney Harbour is a place where people come together, where history and modern life blend seamlessly, and where the beauty of nature is always just a step away.

Sydney Harbour truly is the lifeblood of the city, a place where people from all walks of life gather to work, play, and celebrate. It's a symbol of the city's past, present, and future, and its shimmering waters and vibrant shores continue to inspire everyone who experiences them. Whether you're sailing across its waters, walking along its shores, or simply gazing out at the view, Sydney Harbour offers endless possibilities and an unforgettable experience of life in one of the world's most beautiful cities.

Chapter 9: The Opera House's Iconic White Tiles

The Sydney Opera House is one of the most recognizable buildings in the world, and a big part of what makes it so iconic is its gleaming white tiles that cover the shells. These tiles give the Opera House its unique and stunning appearance, making it look like a shimmering, sail-like structure rising from the waters of Sydney Harbour. But these famous white tiles are not just for decoration—they tell a story of innovation, creativity, and hard work that went into making the Opera House the masterpiece it is today.

The idea for the Sydney Opera House's distinctive white tile design came from its visionary architect, Jørn Utzon. He wanted the building to have a surface that would stand out and sparkle, catching the sunlight during the day and reflecting the moonlight at night. Utzon was inspired by the way light interacts with water, and since the Opera House was being built right on Sydney Harbour, he wanted it to reflect that natural beauty in its design. He imagined a building that looked like it belonged on the water, blending in with the sea and the sky.

But creating tiles that would achieve this effect was no easy task. Utzon and his team of designers and engineers had to figure out how to make tiles that would not only look beautiful but also be strong enough to withstand the harsh conditions of Sydney's climate. The Opera House is right on the edge of the harbor, which means it is constantly exposed to wind, rain, saltwater, and strong sunlight. The tiles needed to be tough enough to endure all of these elements while maintaining their bright white color and smooth finish.

After many months of experimenting, Utzon finally found the perfect solution. Working with a Swedish ceramics company, he developed a special type of tile that was made from crushed stone and glazed with a unique finish. These tiles were designed to be both durable and self-cleaning, meaning they would stay bright and white no matter how much dirt, salt, or pollution built up on them. This was a major breakthrough, as it meant the Opera House wouldn't need constant cleaning and maintenance to keep it looking pristine.

The tiles are not actually pure white, even though they look that way from a distance. Instead, they are a mix of white and cream-colored tiles, with a very subtle pattern that helps to create the shimmering effect Utzon was aiming for. This combination of colors makes the tiles appear to change slightly depending on the time of day and the angle of the sun. In bright sunlight, the tiles can seem to glow, reflecting the blue sky and water around them. At dusk or dawn, they take on a softer, more golden hue as the light changes. And at night, under the lights of the city or the glow of the moon, the Opera House's shells gleam against the dark sky, making it look almost magical.

In total, there are more than one million tiles covering the surface of the Opera House's shells. Each one was carefully placed by hand by skilled workers, ensuring that the pattern and design were perfect. The tiles are arranged in a way that follows the curve of the building's shells, giving the structure its smooth, flowing appearance. The way the tiles are laid is incredibly precise, with each one fitting perfectly next to the others like pieces of a giant jigsaw puzzle.

Because the Opera House is such an iconic landmark, its tiles have become one of its most famous features. People from all over the world come to Sydney just to see the building and its gleaming white sails. The tiles have become a symbol of the Opera House and of Sydney itself—a shining beacon that represents Australia's creativity, innovation, and love of the arts. The building's unique look has inspired artists, architects, and designers for decades, and its influence can be seen in other structures around the world.

One of the most amazing things about the tiles is how they change throughout the day and in different weather conditions. On a sunny day, the tiles can reflect the light so brightly that the building almost seems to glow. On cloudy or rainy days, the tiles take on a softer, more muted look, blending in with the gray skies and making the building feel more mysterious and moody. And after it rains, when the sun comes out and the tiles are still wet, they shimmer even more brightly, reflecting the light like a giant diamond sitting on the harbor.

But the tiles are not just about beauty—they are also an important part of the Opera House's structure. The shells of the building are made from concrete, and without the tiles, they would be rough, dull, and gray. The tiles give the building its smooth, sleek appearance, and they help to protect the concrete underneath from weathering and damage. The unique glaze on the tiles helps to repel water, dirt, and salt, which means that the building stays cleaner and more protected over time.

Even though the tiles are strong and durable, they do require some care and maintenance to keep them looking their best. Over the years, a small number of tiles have been replaced due to damage or wear, but thanks to the high quality of the materials and the skill of the craftsmen who laid them, most of the original tiles are still in place today. This is a testament to the care and attention to detail that went into building the Opera House—every part of the structure, from the grandest shells to the smallest tile, was designed to last.

Visitors to the Sydney Opera House are often surprised to learn just how much thought and effort went into creating the building's famous white tiles. It wasn't just about making the building look beautiful—Utzon and his team wanted to create something that was both functional and artistic, something that would stand the test of time and continue to inspire people for generations to come. The tiles are a perfect example of how great architecture is not just about big ideas, but also about the small details that bring those ideas to life.

When you stand in front of the Opera House and look up at its gleaming white sails, it's easy to see why the building has become one of the most beloved landmarks in the world. The tiles, with their shimmering, almost magical quality, are a big part of what makes the

Opera House so special. They catch the light, reflect the world around them, and change with the time of day and the weather, making the building feel alive, almost like it has its own personality. And while the Opera House may be famous for its grand design, it's the careful craftsmanship of those white tiles that truly brings it to life.

For many people, the Sydney Opera House is not just a building—it's a symbol of hope, creativity, and human achievement. The tiles represent the dedication and hard work of the people who built it, and they remind us that with enough imagination and perseverance, even the most ambitious dreams can become reality. Whether you're looking at the Opera House from across the harbor, walking around its base, or taking a closer look at the intricate patterns of its tiles, you can't help but feel inspired by the beauty and brilliance of this incredible structure. The white tiles of the Sydney Opera House are not just a part of the building—they are a part of its soul.

Chapter 10: The Famous Concert Hall Inside

The Sydney Opera House is known all around the world for its stunning exterior, but what many people don't realize is that inside, it's just as impressive—especially the famous Concert Hall. The Concert Hall is the largest and most spectacular performance space in the Opera House, and it's where some of the greatest musical performances, shows, and events have taken place since the building opened. From its grand design to the amazing sound quality it provides, this hall is a magical place where music and art come to life.

As you enter the Concert Hall, the first thing you notice is how vast it is. With a seating capacity of over 2,500 people, it's like stepping into an enormous, beautiful room that seems to go on forever. The ceiling stretches high above, and the hall itself feels open and airy. The design was made to make everyone feel connected to the performance, no matter where they are sitting. Every seat in the hall offers a fantastic view of the stage, so whether you're right at the front or sitting way in the back, you'll always feel like you're part of the show.

One of the most special things about the Concert Hall is its incredible acoustics. Acoustics are how sound travels in a space, and in the Concert Hall, sound moves perfectly. This is no accident—the architects, engineers, and designers worked very hard to create a hall where music and voices would sound amazing. When a musician plays an instrument or a singer sings a note, the sound bounces off the walls and ceiling in just the right way, filling the entire space without any echoes or muffling. It doesn't matter if it's a delicate note from a violin or a booming chord from an organ—the sound is clear, crisp, and beautiful from every corner of the hall. This perfect sound quality makes the Concert Hall one of the best places in the world to experience live music.

The hall was designed to accommodate all kinds of performances. While it is most famous for its classical music concerts—especially those performed by the Sydney Symphony Orchestra—it is also a stage for opera, ballet, choral performances, and even rock and pop concerts. The flexibility of the space allows it to host a wide variety of shows, from traditional symphonies to contemporary music and experimental performances. The stage can be adapted for different types of performances, whether it's a full orchestra, a solo pianist, or an elaborate opera production.

But one of the most striking features of the Concert Hall is its design. The interior is just as stunning as the exterior of the Opera House. The walls are lined with warm wood paneling that not only looks beautiful but also helps with the acoustics, allowing sound to flow smoothly. The ceiling is made up of giant, curved wooden panels that resemble sails, much like the shells on the outside of the Opera House. These panels not only give the hall a striking, modern look but also play a crucial role in shaping the acoustics. The way they are curved and positioned helps to direct sound evenly throughout the hall, ensuring that every listener hears the performance with perfect clarity.

At the front of the hall, the stage itself is grand and impressive. It's large enough to hold a full orchestra, a choir, and a ballet troupe all at once, giving performers plenty of space to create their art. Behind the stage, towering above everything, is one of the Concert Hall's most iconic features: the grand organ. This is not just any organ—it is the largest mechanical-action pipe organ in the world. With over 10,000 pipes, some of which are as tall as a two-story building, this organ can produce incredibly powerful sounds, from deep, rumbling notes to high, piercing tones. The organ is often used in classical music performances, and when it is played, the entire hall seems to vibrate with its majestic sound.

The seats in the Concert Hall are another example of how much thought went into making this space comfortable and enjoyable for everyone. The seats are cushioned and carefully arranged to give every audience member the best possible view and sound experience. They are positioned in tiers, so even the people sitting at the very back are elevated, giving them a clear view of the stage. The seating design also helps with the acoustics—every seat is positioned in a way that allows sound to reach it perfectly. No matter where you are sitting, you will hear every note and every word as if you were sitting right in front of the stage.

For many people, attending a concert or show in the Sydney Opera House's Concert Hall is a dream come true. The hall has hosted some of the most famous musicians and performers in the world. Legendary conductors, world-class orchestras, and famous singers have all graced the stage, making it a place where history is made with every performance. The Concert Hall has seen everything from grand symphonies to unforgettable solo performances, and every time, the audience is treated to an experience they will never forget.

The lighting inside the Concert Hall adds to its magical atmosphere. Special lighting systems allow the entire space to be lit up in different ways depending on the performance. Sometimes the hall is bathed in soft, warm light for an intimate musical performance, while other times, it is filled with dramatic, colorful lights that match the excitement of a rock concert or a high-energy dance show. The lighting designers work closely with the performers to create just the right mood for every show, making the audience feel like they are part of something truly special.

Another unique feature of the Concert Hall is its connection to the rest of the Sydney Opera House. Before or after a performance, visitors can step outside and take in the breathtaking views of Sydney Harbour. The Opera House is surrounded by water on three sides, and from the Concert Hall, you can walk onto terraces that give you a panoramic view of the harbor, the Sydney Harbour Bridge, and the bustling city beyond. It's a reminder of just how special the location of the Opera

House is, combining world-class performances with one of the most beautiful settings in the world.

Performers who have played in the Concert Hall often speak about what a unique and inspiring space it is. The acoustics, the atmosphere, and the history of the hall make it a dream venue for musicians, singers, and actors alike. Many performers feel a deep sense of honor when they step onto the stage of the Concert Hall, knowing that they are part of a long tradition of world-class performances that have taken place there.

In addition to music and dance performances, the Concert Hall also hosts talks, lectures, and other events. It's a space that brings people together not just to enjoy entertainment but also to learn, share ideas, and celebrate culture. Whether it's a music concert, a theatrical performance, or a speaker series, the Concert Hall is a place where art, knowledge, and inspiration come together in a truly spectacular way.

One of the most memorable aspects of the Concert Hall is how it makes everyone feel—whether you are a performer on stage or a member of the audience, the space has a way of making you feel connected to something bigger than yourself. There's an energy in the air that you can feel as soon as you step inside, a sense that you are about to witness something extraordinary. And because of the Concert Hall's perfect design, every performance feels intimate, no matter how large the audience is. The performers can feel the energy of the crowd, and the audience can feel every emotion in the music or the drama playing out on stage.

Over the years, the Concert Hall has become a symbol of the Opera House itself—a place where creativity, culture, and community come together. It's not just a concert venue—it's a place where memories are made, where people are moved by the power of music, and where the arts are celebrated in their highest form. The Concert Hall is the beating heart of the Sydney Opera House, a place that captures the imagination and leaves everyone who experiences it with a sense of wonder and awe.

In conclusion, the Concert Hall inside the Sydney Opera House is far more than just a room where music is played—it's a masterpiece of architecture and acoustics, a space that brings out the best in every performance. Its grand design, perfect sound, and iconic features like the world's largest pipe organ make it one of the most famous and beloved concert halls in the world. Whether you're attending a classical concert, a rock show, or a ballet, the Concert Hall promises an experience that is truly unforgettable, making it a must-visit destination for anyone who loves the arts.

Chapter 11: The Opera House and Australian Culture

The Sydney Opera House is not just a building; it has become a powerful symbol of Australian culture and identity. From its grand design to its role in the country's artistic scene, the Opera House represents the creativity, innovation, and spirit of Australia. It's a place where people come together to celebrate art, music, dance, theater, and so much more, all while reflecting the rich cultural diversity and history of the country. To understand how the Opera House has influenced and embodied Australian culture, it's important to look at its history, its role in the arts, and how it has connected Australia to the rest of the world.

When the idea for the Sydney Opera House was first imagined, Australia was at a crossroads in terms of how it saw itself on the world stage. The country was growing and evolving, and people wanted a landmark that would showcase their emerging identity to the rest of the world. The decision to build an opera house on Bennelong Point was part of this vision, as it would give Australia a unique and recognizable symbol, much like the Eiffel Tower in Paris or the Statue of Liberty in New York. But unlike these famous structures, the Sydney Opera House was not just an architectural marvel—it was designed to be a functional space for the performing arts, a place where culture and creativity could thrive.

The design of the Opera House itself reflects a deep connection to Australia's natural environment. Architect Jørn Utzon, who designed the building, was inspired by the sails of boats in Sydney Harbour, as well as the natural forms of shells and waves. These curved, flowing shapes give the Opera House a distinctive look that feels both modern and timeless, and they also reflect Australia's coastal heritage. The Opera House's location on the water, surrounded by the stunning beauty of the harbor, adds to its cultural significance—it's a building that could only exist in Australia, capturing the country's unique relationship with the sea, the landscape, and the natural world.

But the Opera House is not just famous for its architecture—it is a place where Australian culture comes to life in many different forms. From the very beginning, the Opera House was intended to be a home for the performing arts, and over the years, it has become a hub for artists, musicians, actors, dancers, and creators from all over the country. It's a place where Australians can experience world-class performances, from classical music to contemporary dance, from opera to rock concerts. The wide range of performances that take place at the Opera House reflects the diversity of Australia's cultural scene, showcasing the talents of local artists while also bringing international performances to Australian audiences.

One of the most important ways the Opera House contributes to Australian culture is by being a space where traditional and modern forms of art come together. Australia is home to a rich Indigenous culture that stretches back tens of thousands of years, and the Opera House has played a role in celebrating and preserving this heritage. Over the years, the Opera House has hosted performances, exhibitions, and events that highlight the art, music, and stories of Australia's Indigenous peoples, offering a platform for their voices to be heard on a global stage. These performances often include traditional dances, songs, and storytelling, but they also explore contemporary Indigenous art forms, blending old and new to create something entirely unique to Australia.

In addition to supporting Indigenous culture, the Opera House has also become a place where multiculturalism is celebrated. Australia is one of the most diverse countries in the world, with people from many different backgrounds calling it home. This diversity is reflected in the performances and events that take place at the Opera House, which often highlight the cultural contributions of the many immigrant communities that have shaped Australia's identity. From Chinese New Year celebrations to Greek theater performances, the Opera House provides a space where different cultures can come together to share their art, music, and traditions with a wider audience.

The Opera House also plays a vital role in shaping the future of Australian culture by supporting new and emerging artists. Through various programs, festivals, and initiatives, the Opera House gives young performers, musicians, and creators a chance to showcase their work. This helps to nurture the next generation of Australian talent, ensuring that the country's cultural scene remains vibrant and dynamic. The Opera House's support for contemporary art forms, such as digital art, experimental theater, and modern music, has allowed it to stay relevant in a rapidly changing world, ensuring that it continues to inspire new ideas and creativity.

Another key aspect of the Opera House's role in Australian culture is its connection to education and community engagement. The Opera House offers a wide range of programs designed to educate and inspire people of all ages, from children to adults. These programs include workshops, performances, and interactive experiences that teach people about the performing arts, as well as the history and significance of the Opera House itself. For many schoolchildren in Australia, visiting the Opera House is a memorable experience that introduces them to the world of art and culture, sparking a lifelong interest in the performing arts. The Opera House's educational initiatives help to build a strong cultural foundation for future generations, ensuring that art and creativity remain central to Australian life.

The Opera House is also a symbol of how Australia sees itself in the global community. When it was completed in 1973, it was one of the most modern and innovative buildings in the world, and it immediately put Australia on the map as a country that embraced bold ideas and new ways of thinking. Today, the Opera House continues to be a symbol of Australia's forward-thinking spirit. It regularly hosts international artists, musicians, and performers, connecting Australia to the global arts scene and allowing Australians to experience the best of what the world has to offer. At the same time, it allows Australian artists to share their work with the world, helping to spread Australian culture to audiences far and wide.

Beyond its role in the arts, the Opera House has also become a symbol of Australian pride and unity. It is a place where Australians gather to celebrate important national events, from New Year's Eve fireworks to Australia Day festivities. The Opera House's iconic sails are often lit up in different colors to mark significant occasions, such as sporting victories, national holidays, or important social causes. This use of the Opera House as a national symbol reflects its deep connection to Australian life—it is not just a building, but a part of the country's collective identity.

Over the years, the Sydney Opera House has also become a powerful symbol of environmental awareness and sustainability in Australia. The Opera House has implemented numerous initiatives to reduce its environmental impact, including energy-efficient lighting, waste reduction programs, and efforts to conserve water. These initiatives reflect Australia's growing commitment to protecting the environment, and they serve as an example of how cultural landmarks can also be leaders in sustainability. The Opera House's dedication to environmental responsibility has inspired other buildings and organizations to follow suit, making it a leader not just in the arts but also in the fight against climate change.

The Opera House's place in Australian culture is also evident in the way it is portrayed in the media, literature, and popular culture. It is one of the most photographed buildings in the world, and its image is instantly recognizable. It has been featured in countless films, television shows, books, and advertisements, often serving as a symbol of Australia itself. For many people around the world, the sight of the Opera House immediately brings to mind images of Australia's natural beauty, its vibrant cities, and its rich cultural scene. The building has become so iconic that it is often used to represent Australia in international media, making it a powerful symbol of the country's identity.

For tourists visiting Australia, the Opera House is often at the top of their list of places to see. Millions of people visit the Opera House every year, not just to see a performance but also to experience the beauty and history of the building itself. Guided tours take visitors behind the scenes, offering them a glimpse into the inner workings of the Opera House and allowing them to learn about its history, architecture, and cultural significance. For many visitors, a trip to the Opera House is a way to connect with Australian culture and gain a deeper understanding of the country's artistic heritage.

In conclusion, the Sydney Opera House is much more than just a landmark—it is a living, breathing part of Australian culture. It represents the country's creativity, diversity, and forward-thinking spirit, while also serving as a hub for the performing arts. Through its support of Indigenous and multicultural art forms, its commitment to nurturing new talent, and its role in the global arts scene, the Opera House continues to shape and reflect the culture of Australia. It is a place where people come together to celebrate music, dance, theater, and more, and it has become a symbol of the country's unique identity and its connection to the world. The Sydney Opera House is not just a building; it is a cultural icon that will continue to inspire and unite Australians for generations to come.

Chapter 12: Night Lights and Special Events

The Sydney Opera House at night is one of the most magical sights you could ever imagine. When the sun sets, and the sky turns dark, the building transforms into something truly spectacular. Its famous white sails light up, reflecting the surrounding harbor and glowing under the stars. But it's not just the lights that make the Opera House so special at night—it's also home to some of the most exciting and creative events you can think of. From festivals and concerts to light shows and celebrations, the Opera House becomes a place of wonder and excitement after dark.

One of the most amazing things about the Sydney Opera House at night is how it uses lights to create different moods and atmospheres. The Opera House is known for its brilliant lighting displays, where the sails are covered with colorful images and patterns that seem to dance and move across the surface. These displays aren't just about making the building look pretty; they're often designed to tell stories, celebrate important occasions, or highlight special events happening in Australia and around the world. For instance, during Vivid Sydney, an annual festival of light, music, and ideas, the Opera House becomes a canvas for incredible light projections that captivate people from all over the globe.

Vivid Sydney is one of the most popular events at the Opera House, and it transforms the building into a dazzling spectacle of color and light. Artists from around the world are invited to create light displays that cover the sails with images that are both beautiful and thought-provoking. These light projections can include anything from animals and nature scenes to abstract patterns and animations that move and change with the music. Vivid Sydney isn't just about watching lights; it's an interactive experience where visitors can walk around and explore the light installations that are set up all around the harbor and the city. The Opera House is always the centerpiece of the event, and people come from far and wide just to see how the building is lit up each year.

But Vivid Sydney is just one example of how the Opera House comes alive at night. Throughout the year, the building hosts special events that bring together people from all walks of life to enjoy the arts, music, and culture. These events are often held under the stars or inside the beautifully lit concert halls, making them feel even more magical. For instance, during New Year's Eve, the Opera House is one of the most popular spots in the world to watch fireworks. Thousands of people gather around Sydney Harbour to celebrate the new year, and the Opera House is lit up in spectacular colors, with fireworks exploding over its sails and reflecting off the water. It's a sight that people look forward to all year long, and it's broadcast on television around the world, making the Opera House a symbol of celebration and joy.

The Opera House is also known for lighting up its sails to mark important national and international events. For example, on Australia Day, the sails are often lit up in the colors of the Australian flag, creating a patriotic display that makes people feel proud to be part of the country's culture and history. On other occasions, the sails are illuminated to support causes like environmental awareness, human rights, or health campaigns. This use of lighting helps to connect the Opera House with events that matter to people, both in Australia and around the world, turning the building into a beacon of hope, unity, and solidarity.

One of the most moving lighting displays occurs on ANZAC Day, a national day of remembrance in Australia and New Zealand to honor the members of the armed forces who served in wars, conflicts, and peacekeeping operations. On this day, the sails of the Opera House may be lit with images of poppies or other symbols of remembrance, creating a solemn and respectful tribute to those who have served the country. The lights create a quiet, reflective atmosphere, reminding everyone of the sacrifices made by brave individuals in the past.

In addition to light shows, the Opera House is also home to special performances and events that make nighttime visits truly unforgettable. The building hosts outdoor concerts and theater performances under the stars, where audiences can enjoy world-class music and drama with the city skyline and the illuminated sails of the Opera House as a backdrop. These events are often part of festivals or seasonal celebrations, such as the Sydney Festival, which takes place in January each year. The Sydney Festival brings a wide range of performances to the Opera House, including live music, dance, and theater, all set against the stunning night views of the harbor.

During the warmer months, the Opera House's forecourt and outdoor spaces are used for open-air cinema screenings, where visitors can watch movies under the night sky with the Opera House and the Sydney Harbour Bridge in the background. These events are perfect for families, friends, and visitors looking to experience something different and exciting while enjoying the beauty of the Opera House at night. There's something magical about sitting outside, with the cool evening breeze and the lights of the city twinkling around you, while the Opera House glows in the distance.

The Opera House also plays a key role in Sydney's New Year's Eve celebrations. As one of the world's most famous New Year's Eve destinations, Sydney attracts hundreds of thousands of visitors to its harbor to watch the spectacular fireworks display. The Opera House serves as a backdrop to this grand celebration, and its sails are often lit up in colorful patterns that change throughout the night. The fireworks light up the sky and reflect off the water, creating a breathtaking scene that is broadcast to millions of people around the world. For many, seeing the Opera House lit up during the New Year's Eve fireworks is a bucket-list experience, and it's a night that people remember for years to come.

Another popular event that takes place at night is the annual Lunar New Year celebrations. During this time, the Opera House is often lit up with red and gold colors, symbolizing good luck and prosperity for the coming year. The Opera House hosts special performances and cultural events to celebrate the Lunar New Year, with a focus on Chinese, Korean, and Vietnamese traditions. Visitors can enjoy lion dances, music performances, and traditional food as they take in the sights of the Opera House glowing in festive colors.

The Opera House also offers nighttime tours that give visitors a behind-the-scenes look at the building when it's all lit up. These tours allow people to explore the inside of the Opera House, visiting areas that are normally off-limits to the public, such as the backstage areas of the theaters and concert halls. The tours often include stories about the history of the building, its architecture, and its role in Australian culture, and they offer a chance to see the Opera House in a whole new light—quite literally!

For those interested in dance, the Opera House hosts special ballet and dance performances that are often scheduled in the evening. These performances take place in the Opera House's grand theaters, where the stage is illuminated with beautiful lighting that enhances the drama and beauty of the dance. Watching a ballet or contemporary dance performance inside the Opera House at night is an experience that's hard to describe—it feels like you're part of something truly magical, surrounded by art and beauty on all sides.

Beyond performances, the Opera House is also home to nighttime art exhibitions and installations. Throughout the year, the building hosts exhibitions of visual art, sculpture, and photography, often showcasing the work of Australian and international artists. Some of these exhibitions take place outdoors, where the art is illuminated by special lighting that makes it come alive under the night sky. Visitors can stroll around the Opera House, taking in the art and the views of the harbor, all while the sails of the building glow in the distance.

Even ordinary nights at the Opera House can feel extraordinary. The way the building lights up the harbor, casting reflections on the water, creates a peaceful and enchanting atmosphere. Whether you're attending a performance, exploring the area, or simply enjoying the view from across the harbor, the Opera House at night is a sight that leaves a lasting impression. The lighting, the events, and the sense of celebration that fills the air all combine to make the Opera House a truly unforgettable place after the sun goes down.

In conclusion, the Sydney Opera House is not just a place to visit during the day—it's a building that comes alive at night, with its brilliant lighting displays, special events, and performances creating an atmosphere of wonder and excitement. From the spectacular light shows of Vivid Sydney to the fireworks of New Year's Eve, the Opera House is a central part of Sydney's nighttime celebrations and a symbol of creativity, culture, and joy. Whether it's through art, music, dance, or simply the way it lights up the harbor, the Opera House is a place where magic happens after dark, and it's a place that will continue to inspire awe and wonder for generations to come.

Chapter 13: Wildlife Around the Opera House

The Sydney Opera House might be one of the most famous buildings in the world, but it's not just people who enjoy its surroundings. The area around the Opera House, including the waters of Sydney Harbour and the nearby Royal Botanic Garden, is teeming with wildlife. These creatures, big and small, make the Opera House and its surroundings an even more fascinating place to explore. From the sea to the skies, the wildlife around the Opera House brings the area to life in ways that many visitors might not expect.

One of the most interesting parts of the Opera House's location is its close connection to the water. The Opera House sits right on the edge of Sydney Harbour, and the water here is home to a variety of marine animals. If you're lucky, you might spot some of the harbor's most famous residents—bottlenose dolphins. These playful creatures are often seen swimming and leaping through the waves, sometimes right in front of the Opera House. Dolphins love to follow boats and often put on a show for anyone watching. Their sleek, silvery bodies can be seen cutting through the water as they jump and splash, delighting both locals and visitors.

In addition to dolphins, Sydney Harbour is also home to a variety of fish species. The clear waters around the Opera House are teeming with different kinds of fish, from small schools of silverfish to larger species like kingfish and snapper. The fish are attracted to the harbor's underwater vegetation and structures, which provide food and shelter. Some visitors to the Opera House might even spot anglers along the waterfront, casting their lines in hopes of catching something fresh from the sea. The harbor is also a great place to see other marine animals like rays, which glide gracefully through the water with their wide, flat bodies. Although they might look a little intimidating, rays are generally peaceful creatures and can often be seen near the shallow waters around the Opera House.

The Opera House's position on the harbor means it's also a great place for birdwatching. Seagulls are some of the most common birds you'll see here, circling in the sky or perched on the nearby docks and piers. They swoop down to catch food scraps and can often be heard squawking as they patrol the harbor. But seagulls are just the beginning. The skies around the Opera House are also home to more majestic birds like pelicans and cormorants. Pelicans are known for their enormous beaks and wingspans. These graceful birds can often be seen gliding above the water before plunging down to catch fish. Cormorants, on the other hand, are excellent divers. They're often spotted perched on rocks or piers with their wings spread wide as they dry off after diving underwater for fish.

For a closer look at the wildlife on land, a visit to the Royal Botanic Garden, which is right next to the Opera House, is a must. This lush, green oasis is full of native Australian plants, and it's a haven for birds, insects, and other small animals. As you wander through the gardens, you might hear the calls of kookaburras, a type of bird famous for its laughing call. Kookaburras are part of the kingfisher family, and they're easy to spot with their distinctive white and brown feathers. They're known to be very vocal, especially in the early mornings and late afternoons, filling the gardens with their unique laughter-like calls.

Another bird you're likely to encounter in the Botanic Garden is the colorful rainbow lorikeet. These small parrots are a sight to behold with their bright green, blue, red, and yellow feathers. They are often seen flying in pairs or small flocks, chattering loudly as they flit from tree to tree. They love to feed on nectar from flowers, so you might catch them hanging upside down from branches as they drink from blossoms. Their vibrant colors and playful behavior make them one of the most delightful sights in the area.

The Botanic Garden is also home to many ibis birds, which are a common sight around Sydney. These tall, long-beaked birds are often seen walking around the gardens or along the waterfront near the Opera House. With their white feathers and curved black beaks, they're hard to miss. Ibis birds are scavengers, which means they'll often poke around in the grass or near picnic areas looking for food. While some people find them a bit pesky, they play an important role in the local ecosystem by helping to clean up waste and debris.

If you take a closer look in the gardens, you might also spot smaller creatures like skinks and other types of lizards. These little reptiles love to bask in the sun on warm days and can often be seen darting across rocks or along the garden paths. They're quick and often hide among the plants, but with patience, you can spot them warming themselves in sunny spots. The Royal Botanic Garden is also home to several types of frogs, which live in the ponds and wetlands within the gardens. On quiet evenings, you can often hear the croaking of frogs echoing through the area, a reminder of the rich wildlife that lives alongside this famous landmark.

At night, the wildlife around the Opera House becomes even more fascinating. As the sun sets and the lights of the Opera House begin to glow, nocturnal creatures come out to explore. One of the most interesting nighttime visitors is the flying fox, a type of bat that can be seen swooping through the air after dark. Flying foxes are large fruit bats, and they're often spotted in the trees near the Botanic Garden or flying over the harbor in search of food. With their wide wingspans and silent flight, they're a bit mysterious, but they play an important role in pollinating plants and dispersing seeds throughout the area.

Another nocturnal animal that can be found in the area is the possum. Possums are small marsupials with bushy tails, and they're common in Australian cities. At night, you might see them climbing trees or sneaking through the gardens in search of food. Possums are curious creatures, and they're often spotted near the Opera House, especially in areas with plenty of trees or vegetation. While they're mostly active at night, you can sometimes catch a glimpse of them resting in trees during the day.

Beyond the Opera House and the Botanic Garden, the waters of Sydney Harbour are also home to some larger marine creatures. During certain times of the year, visitors might be lucky enough to spot whales as they migrate along the coast of Australia. Humpback whales, in particular, are known for their impressive migrations and are often seen breaching and splashing in the waters near Sydney. While they're more commonly spotted further out at sea, on special occasions, whales have been seen closer to the Opera House, thrilling visitors with their powerful displays.

In addition to whales, sharks are also present in Sydney Harbour, although they're not commonly seen near the Opera House. The harbor is home to several species of sharks, including the harmless Port Jackson shark, which spends much of its time on the ocean floor, and the wobbegong, a type of shark that blends in with the rocky seabed. These sharks are more active in deeper waters, so they're not often seen near the shore, but knowing they're part of the harbor's ecosystem adds to the sense of adventure around the Opera House.

Insects also play a role in the wildlife around the Opera House. During the warmer months, you might notice butterflies fluttering around the Botanic Garden, attracted to the vibrant flowers that grow there. Dragonflies and bees are also common sights, buzzing around the plants and helping with pollination. While insects might seem small and easy to overlook, they are an essential part of the natural world that surrounds the Opera House, contributing to the health of the plants and the overall ecosystem.

In conclusion, the wildlife around the Sydney Opera House is as diverse and vibrant as the building itself. From the dolphins and fish in the harbor to the birds and insects in the Royal Botanic Garden, there's a rich variety of animals that call this area home. Whether you're watching pelicans glide over the water or listening to the laughter of kookaburras in the trees, the animals around the Opera House bring a special kind of life and energy to this iconic landmark. Exploring the area's wildlife adds another layer of wonder to any visit, reminding us that nature and culture can thrive side by side in one of the world's most beautiful settings.

Chapter 14: Sydney's Opera House and the World Stage

The Sydney Opera House is much more than just a building; it's a symbol of Australia and one of the most recognized landmarks in the world. But beyond its stunning design and unique shape, the Opera House plays a crucial role in connecting Australia to the world through the arts. It stands as a cultural beacon, where performers from all corners of the globe gather to share their talents with audiences. Whether it's a grand opera, an electrifying rock concert, or a moving ballet performance, the Opera House has hosted some of the most iconic events on the world stage, making it a vital part of the international arts community.

From the moment it opened in 1973, the Sydney Opera House became a symbol of artistic ambition, not just for Australia, but for the world. Its architecture, created by Danish architect Jørn Utzon, was so revolutionary that people from across the globe were drawn to it. The Opera House quickly earned a reputation as one of the best places to perform, and top musicians, dancers, and actors began traveling to Sydney to showcase their work in this magnificent venue. Performers were inspired by the building's beauty and history, knowing that performing on its stage was a huge honor.

But what truly makes the Sydney Opera House stand out is the variety of events it hosts. It's not just home to traditional opera or classical music, though those are still a huge part of its identity. Over the years, the Opera House has opened its doors to all types of performances. World-renowned orchestras like the Berlin Philharmonic and the New York Philharmonic have filled its concert halls with rich, powerful music. Famous singers like Luciano Pavarotti, the legendary Italian tenor, have performed operas in its grand spaces, while international pop stars like Adele and Beyoncé have lit up the stage with unforgettable concerts.

In addition to concerts, the Sydney Opera House is a favorite venue for global theatre companies. Plays that have taken the world by storm, such as those from London's West End or New York's Broadway, have made their way to Sydney. These productions bring stories from around the world to Australian audiences and introduce the country's culture to international visitors. The mix of international and local talent creates a special blend that ensures the Opera House continues to be an influential player on the global stage.

One of the most exciting aspects of the Opera House's role on the world stage is its connection to the world of dance. The building is home to the Australian Ballet, one of the world's leading ballet companies, and it often hosts performances by international dance troupes. Whether it's traditional ballet performances like "Swan Lake" or contemporary dance productions that push the boundaries of movement, the Opera House is known for showcasing the best of the dance world. Dance companies from countries like Russia, France, and the United States regularly perform here, bringing the global language of dance to Sydney.

Festivals are another major way the Opera House connects to the world stage. Throughout the year, the Opera House hosts a wide range of festivals that attract artists and audiences from all over the globe. The Sydney Festival, for example, is a major event held every January, featuring performances in music, theatre, dance, and more. Artists from across the world come to participate, making it a celebration of global talent. Another major event is Vivid Sydney, a spectacular light, music, and ideas festival that transforms the Opera House into a canvas for vibrant light displays. During Vivid, international artists collaborate with local creators to put on one of the most impressive visual displays in the world. The Opera House's sails are lit up with stunning images, and the whole of Sydney Harbour comes alive with color and creativity.

In addition to its role as a stage for performers, the Opera House is also a place for big, important conversations. Every year, the Opera House hosts talks and conferences where some of the world's most influential thinkers, writers, and scientists gather to discuss important issues. These events bring together people from around the world to share ideas and solutions for the challenges we all face. Speakers like Nobel Prize winners, world leaders, and famous authors have spoken at the Opera House, making it a place where big ideas come to life.

Perhaps one of the most amazing things about the Sydney Opera House is how it represents the global nature of the arts while also staying deeply connected to its Australian roots. The Opera House has played a crucial role in showcasing Australian talent on the world stage. Local musicians, playwrights, dancers, and artists see the Opera House as the ultimate venue to perform and show their work to the world. Many Australian artists who have gone on to become famous internationally, such as the opera singer Joan Sutherland and the rock band INXS, have had unforgettable performances at the Opera House. For them, the Opera House is both a home and a gateway to the world.

The Opera House's influence extends beyond just performances. Its status as a UNESCO World Heritage site places it among some of the world's most treasured landmarks. This recognition means that the Sydney Opera House is considered of outstanding value to humanity, on par with sites like the Great Wall of China and the Pyramids of Egypt. Being listed as a UNESCO World Heritage site also helps the Opera House attract more global attention, drawing tourists and art lovers from all corners of the earth who want to experience its beauty and history firsthand. For many people, visiting the Opera House is a dream come true. Whether they're attending a performance or simply standing on its steps and admiring the view, people from all over the world are captivated by this architectural masterpiece.

One of the key ways the Opera House continues to engage with the world is through technology. In today's digital age, the Opera House is committed to bringing its performances to global audiences, even if they can't visit in person. Many concerts, ballets, and talks are live-streamed, allowing people from around the world to experience the magic of the Opera House from the comfort of their homes. This use of technology has opened up new possibilities for how the Opera House connects to the world stage, making it even more accessible to international audiences. Whether you're in Sydney or on the other side of the world, you can still enjoy the world-class performances that take place in this iconic venue.

The Opera House is also a symbol of Australia's place in the world. It's a building that represents the creativity, openness, and diversity of the country. Sydney is a multicultural city, and the Opera House reflects this in the range of performances and events it hosts. Whether it's a performance of traditional Aboriginal music and dance, or an international music festival, the Opera House is a place where cultures from all over the world come together. It's a symbol of how Australia is connected to the global community and how the arts can bring people together, no matter where they come from.

Finally, the Opera House's role on the world stage goes beyond the performances and events it hosts. It's also a place of inspiration. Architects, artists, and performers from around the world have been inspired by the Sydney Opera House and its daring design. Its unique shape and location have influenced countless buildings and cultural spaces across the globe. The Opera House reminds people that creativity has no limits and that with bold ideas, we can create something that touches the hearts and minds of people everywhere.

In conclusion, Sydney's Opera House is a powerful symbol of the arts, both in Australia and around the world. Its stages have welcomed the most talented performers, and its halls have echoed with the voices of the most influential thinkers. The Opera House brings the world together through the arts, connecting people and cultures in a way that few other places can. Whether it's through a thrilling concert, a moving dance performance, or a thoughtful conversation, the Opera House continues to be a beacon of global culture, standing proudly on the edge of Sydney Harbour, welcoming the world to its doors.

Chapter 15: Fun Facts About the Opera House Design

The Sydney Opera House is one of the most famous buildings in the world, and it's not just because of its stunning location on Sydney Harbour. What makes it so special is its incredibly unique design, which has captured the imagination of people all over the world. The Opera House's design is so creative and daring that it's often seen as a masterpiece of modern architecture. But behind its beauty, there are many fascinating and fun facts about how this amazing structure came to be and what makes its design so extraordinary.

First, let's talk about the shape of the Opera House. The building is most famous for its roof, which looks like a series of giant white shells or sails. These shells seem to float above the water, making the Opera House look like it's ready to set sail across the harbour. But did you know that when the Danish architect Jørn Utzon first imagined the design, he didn't think of shells or sails at all? His original inspiration came from the idea of nature itself. Utzon was fascinated by the curves and shapes found in nature, like the wings of a bird or the peeling of an orange. In fact, after many designs, he settled on the idea that the shells should all be parts of a perfect sphere, like slices from a peeled orange. This gave the Opera House its distinct, geometric look. It's incredible to think that such an iconic building could be inspired by something as simple and natural as an orange!

Another fun fact about the design is that it was chosen through an international competition. Back in the 1950s, Sydney was looking for a bold new design for a performing arts center, and they invited architects from all over the world to submit their ideas. There were 233 entries from 32 different countries, and Utzon's design was one of the last to be considered. At first, some of the judges weren't even sure what to make of it because it was so unusual and different from the other entries. But one of the judges, the famous architect Eero Saarinen, saw the potential in Utzon's vision and insisted that it be chosen. Thanks to his keen eye, Utzon's daring design was selected, and the rest is history. It just goes to show how one person's vision can change everything!

One of the most interesting things about the Opera House's design is how hard it was to build. When Jørn Utzon first came up with the idea for the shell-shaped roof, no one had ever built anything like it before. In fact, the engineers working on the project weren't sure it was even possible to build such a complex structure. The shells had to be made from huge sections of concrete, and each one needed to be precisely shaped to fit together perfectly. The construction team had to invent brand-new techniques and use cutting-edge technology just to figure out how to make it work. It took years of trial and error, and some people even thought the project might have to be abandoned because it was so difficult. But eventually, through hard work and determination, the team found a way to bring Utzon's vision to life.

One of the coolest things about the Opera House is that it's not just beautiful to look at – it's also incredibly functional. The shells on the roof are designed to not only create an iconic shape but also to provide protection from the sun and rain. The sails are positioned in such a way that they help keep the building cool during the hot Australian summers by allowing air to circulate between them. And the white tiles that cover the roof are specially designed to reflect the sunlight, making the Opera House shimmer in the daylight without getting too hot. In fact, the tiles themselves are an engineering marvel. There are over one million tiles on the roof, and they were all made in Sweden because they needed to be both durable and reflective. These tiles give the Opera House its famous white, gleaming appearance, and from a distance, they make it look almost like a sculpture rising from the water.

Speaking of the tiles, here's a fun fact that many people don't know: the white tiles aren't actually all white! If you look closely, you'll see that the tiles are made up of two different shades: glossy white and matte cream. This clever combination of colors creates the perfect balance of shine and texture, making the roof look bright and reflective without being blinding in the sun. The next time you see a picture of the Opera House, or if you're lucky enough to visit in person, you can look closely at the tiles and see this incredible detail for yourself.

Another fascinating part of the Opera House's design is its location. Utzon carefully chose the site on Bennelong Point because he wanted the building to be as close to the water as possible. The location allows the Opera House to be surrounded by water on three sides, which makes it look like it's floating on the harbour. The design also takes full advantage of Sydney's beautiful natural scenery, with stunning views of the Harbour Bridge and the skyline of the city. When you stand in front of the Opera House, it feels like you're at the center of Sydney's most breathtaking sights.

The design of the Opera House wasn't just about how it looked from the outside, though. Utzon also paid close attention to the interiors and how the building would function for performers and audiences. Inside the Opera House, there are several different performance spaces, each one designed to enhance the experience of listening to music, watching a play, or enjoying a dance performance. The largest space, the Concert Hall, is known for its incredible acoustics, which means that sound travels perfectly throughout the room, allowing the audience to hear every note clearly, no matter where they're sitting. Utzon worked with acoustics experts to ensure that the design would create the best possible sound quality, making the Concert Hall one of the most famous music venues in the world.

One of the fun facts about the Opera House's design is that it was so ahead of its time that Jørn Utzon never actually saw it fully completed. Although Utzon left the project before it was finished due to disagreements with the local government, his vision was so strong that the team that took over continued to follow his design principles.

Years later, Utzon's son, Jan Utzon, who is also an architect, worked on some updates to the Opera House, bringing the building even closer to his father's original vision. In a way, it's like the design of the Opera House is a family legacy, passed down from father to son.

The Opera House's design has also had a huge influence on architecture around the world. Its bold, modern style inspired architects to think differently about how buildings could look and function. Instead of just focusing on practicality, architects began to see buildings as works of art, where beauty and creativity were just as important as strength and durability. Today, many famous buildings, such as the Guggenheim Museum in New York and the Lotus Temple in India, draw inspiration from the daring and innovative design of the Sydney Opera House.

Another fun fact about the design is that the Opera House has become a symbol of Australia itself. When people think of Sydney, the first image that often comes to mind is the Opera House with its iconic sails. It's a building that represents not just the city but the entire country. In fact, the Sydney Opera House is so beloved that it has appeared on Australian currency and stamps. It's even been declared a UNESCO World Heritage Site, which means it's considered one of the most important cultural landmarks in the world.

Finally, the design of the Opera House continues to evolve and inspire new generations. Even today, architects and designers study Jørn Utzon's work to learn about the incredible balance between form and function. The Opera House remains a place of creativity, where new ideas in architecture and design are celebrated. Every year, during the Vivid Sydney festival, the sails of the Opera House are transformed into a canvas for light shows, with colorful and artistic designs projected onto the building, bringing it to life in new and exciting ways.

In conclusion, the design of the Sydney Opera House is full of fun and fascinating details that make it one of the most remarkable buildings in the world. From its unique shell-shaped roof inspired by nature to its incredible engineering feats, every part of the Opera House tells a story of creativity, innovation, and beauty. It's a building that has captured the hearts of people all over the world, and its design continues to inspire and amaze visitors, architects, and artists alike.

Chapter 16: Famous Performances at the Opera House

The Sydney Opera House is one of the world's most famous performance venues, and over the years, it has hosted countless incredible shows and events that have thrilled audiences from all around the globe. The performances that take place here are as legendary as the building itself. From world-class concerts to breathtaking ballets, captivating operas to dramatic plays, the Opera House has been a stage for some of the most unforgettable and famous performances in history. Let's dive into the fascinating world of the shows that have made the Sydney Opera House a symbol of creativity, artistry, and culture.

One of the first things you should know about the Sydney Opera House is that it isn't just a place for one type of performance. While the word "opera" is in its name, the Opera House is actually home to a wide range of art forms, including opera, classical music, modern dance, contemporary theater, comedy, and even rock and pop concerts. This variety is one of the reasons the Opera House is so beloved—it's a space where artists of all kinds can come together to share their work with audiences.

One of the most famous performances in the history of the Opera House took place during its grand opening in 1973. The opening was celebrated with a royal performance attended by Queen Elizabeth II herself, who officially opened the building. During this special event, there were performances by the Australian Opera and the Sydney Symphony Orchestra, showcasing the Opera House's incredible acoustics and its ability to host world-class musical events. This grand celebration set the stage for decades of famous performances that followed.

Over the years, many legendary opera singers have graced the stage at the Sydney Opera House. One of the most famous was Luciano Pavarotti, one of the greatest tenors of all time. Pavarotti's powerful voice filled the Opera House's Concert Hall during several performances, creating unforgettable moments for everyone lucky enough to be in the audience. His performances at the Opera House are still talked about today as some of the most magical in the venue's history.

Another unforgettable opera performance was "Turandot" by Giacomo Puccini, a grand and dramatic production that captivated audiences with its stunning costumes, set designs, and, of course, the incredible music. The Opera House's main theater, the Joan Sutherland Theatre, has hosted countless opera productions like "Carmen," "La Traviata," and "Madame Butterfly," each one bringing to life the timeless stories and beautiful music that opera lovers cherish.

But the Opera House isn't just for opera. It has also been the site of many amazing ballet performances, with the Australian Ballet frequently performing here. One of the most famous ballets to be performed at the Opera House is "Swan Lake." This classic ballet, with its graceful movements and hauntingly beautiful music by Tchaikovsky, has been performed multiple times at the Opera House, enchanting audiences with its tale of love, magic, and tragedy. The stunning choreography, paired with the elegance of the dancers, has made every performance of "Swan Lake" at the Opera House a masterpiece.

In addition to opera and ballet, the Sydney Opera House has also hosted some of the world's greatest orchestras. The Sydney Symphony Orchestra performs regularly at the Opera House, filling the Concert Hall with the sounds of symphonic masterpieces by composers like Beethoven, Mozart, and Mahler. One of the most famous performances was when conductor Leonard Bernstein led the orchestra in a powerful rendition of Beethoven's Ninth Symphony. The grandeur of the music combined with the iconic setting of the Opera House made this performance one for the history books.

And then there are the famous plays and theater performances that have been staged at the Opera House. The Sydney Theatre Company, one of Australia's most prestigious theater companies, frequently performs at the Opera House, showcasing a wide range of productions from Shakespearean classics to contemporary dramas. One of the most famous performances was Cate Blanchett's portrayal of Hedda Gabler in Henrik Ibsen's play of the same name. Her powerful performance was praised by critics and audiences alike, further cementing the Opera House's reputation as a world-class venue for theater.

In addition to high culture like opera, ballet, and theater, the Sydney Opera House has also been a stage for more modern and popular forms of entertainment. Rock and pop concerts have become a beloved part of the Opera House's offerings, drawing huge crowds of music fans. One of the most famous rock performances was by the band Crowded House, who played an iconic farewell concert on the steps of the Opera House in 1996. The concert, called "Farewell to the World," was attended by over 100,000 people and broadcast to millions more. This performance is remembered as one of the greatest in Australian music history, and it showcased the Opera House as a venue that can host events on an epic scale.

Another major musical moment was when legendary singer-songwriter Bob Dylan performed at the Opera House. His concert was a major event, attracting fans from all over the world to hear his iconic voice and timeless songs in such a prestigious setting. Similarly, American artist Prince gave a legendary performance at the Opera House during his 2012 tour. These concerts demonstrated the Opera House's ability to host not only classical performances but also rock and pop music legends.

Comedy has also found a home at the Sydney Opera House, with famous comedians performing stand-up routines that have left audiences in stitches. Some of the world's top comedians, including John Cleese, Jerry Seinfeld, and Chris Rock, have performed at the Opera House, proving that it's a place where all forms of entertainment can shine.

In addition to individual performances, the Sydney Opera House is home to many special events and festivals. One of the most famous events is Vivid Sydney, a festival of light, music, and ideas. During this festival, the sails of the Opera House are lit up with stunning light projections, creating a visual spectacle that attracts visitors from all over the world. The festival also includes concerts and performances, making it one of the most exciting times of the year at the Opera House.

Film premieres and screenings have also been a highlight of the Opera House's events. It has hosted special premieres for major movies, including some of the "Star Wars" films, with the Concert Hall being transformed into a movie theater for the occasion. These events bring together movie stars, directors, and fans in a celebration of cinema.

Another fascinating aspect of the Opera House's performance history is the number of international artists and performers who have traveled from all corners of the globe to showcase their talents in Sydney. The Opera House's international reputation means that it attracts some of the most famous artists, dancers, musicians, and actors from around the world, making it a true hub of global culture. From the New York Philharmonic to the Bolshoi Ballet, the Opera House has hosted performances by some of the most prestigious artistic institutions on the planet.

One of the reasons these performances are so unforgettable is because of the Opera House's stunning setting. There's something magical about watching a live performance while being surrounded by the beauty of Sydney Harbour. Whether it's a night at the opera, a ballet, or a rock concert, the combination of world-class performances and breathtaking scenery makes every event at the Opera House feel like a once-in-a-lifetime experience.

In recent years, the Opera House has embraced digital technology to bring performances to an even larger audience. With live-streamed concerts and virtual events, people from all over the world can now experience the magic of the Sydney Opera House without ever leaving their homes. This has allowed the Opera House to continue its tradition of hosting famous and exciting performances while reaching new audiences globally.

To sum it all up, the Sydney Opera House has been the stage for some of the most famous and diverse performances in the world. From legendary opera singers to rock stars, from breathtaking ballets to cutting-edge theater, the Opera House has hosted it all. The incredible variety of performances, combined with the stunning beauty of the building and its surroundings, has made the Opera House a symbol of artistic excellence and cultural importance. Whether it's a grand opera, a rock concert under the stars, or a film premiere, the Sydney Opera House continues to be a place where unforgettable performances happen every day, bringing joy, inspiration, and wonder to audiences from all over the globe.

Chapter 17: How the Opera House Stays So Clean

The Sydney Opera House is one of the most iconic buildings in the world, instantly recognizable for its stunning white shells that seem to rise from the waters of Sydney Harbour. When people think about this landmark, they often picture it gleaming in the bright Australian sunlight, its surfaces sparkling and clean. But have you ever wondered how the Opera House stays so clean? Keeping such a large and complex structure looking spotless is no easy task, especially when it's exposed to harsh weather conditions, sea spray, and the sheer number of visitors who come to admire it each year. The process of maintaining the Opera House's cleanliness is a fascinating story of dedication, hard work, and some pretty amazing techniques and tools.

Let's start by talking about the tiles that cover the Sydney Opera House's famous shells. There are over a million tiles on the roof, and they come in two colors—glossy white and matte cream. These tiles are arranged in a way that gives the Opera House its signature look, reflecting light beautifully and making the building shine from different angles. The tiles were designed to be self-cleaning to some extent. Because they are made from a special material, dirt and dust don't stick to them easily. When it rains, the water naturally washes away much of the dirt, keeping the tiles looking fresh. This was one of the smart design choices made by the Opera House's architect, Jørn Utzon, and his team, who knew that maintaining such a large surface would be challenging.

However, relying on rain to keep the tiles clean isn't enough to maintain the Opera House's spotless appearance. The building is located right on the edge of Sydney Harbour, where salty sea spray and the wind can bring a lot of grime and pollution to its surface. Over time, the salt from the ocean and other pollutants in the air can cause a buildup of dirt on the tiles, making them look dull and dingy. To prevent this, the Opera House needs regular cleaning to keep it looking as spectacular as the day it opened.

One of the most interesting things about cleaning the Sydney Opera House is that it can't be done in a traditional way. For example, you can't just send people up with buckets of soapy water and scrubbing brushes to clean the shells. The surface is too large and too curved, making it difficult for workers to reach all the areas safely. Instead, specialized teams are brought in to clean the tiles, and they use state-of-the-art equipment to do the job.

High-pressure water jets are one of the tools used to clean the Opera House's roof. These powerful jets spray water at a very high pressure, which helps to remove any dirt, salt, or pollution that has built up on the tiles. The great thing about using water jets is that they don't require any harsh chemicals, so they are environmentally friendly and won't damage the tiles. The pressure of the water is carefully controlled to ensure that it cleans effectively without harming the tiles or the grout that holds them in place.

In addition to high-pressure water jets, other techniques are used for more stubborn dirt or areas that are harder to reach. Sometimes, workers need to use ropes and harnesses to rappel down the side of the Opera House's sails. These highly trained professionals, known as abseilers, dangle from ropes and use specialized cleaning tools to scrub away dirt and grime. It's a job that requires both skill and courage, as the abseilers must navigate the Opera House's steep, curved surfaces while cleaning every inch of the structure.

For areas of the Opera House that are especially difficult to access, like the highest points of the sails, remote-controlled cleaning robots have been developed. These robots are equipped with brushes and other cleaning tools, and they can move across the tiles to reach spots that human workers might find too dangerous. The use of robots not only helps with efficiency but also ensures that no part of the Opera House's surface is left dirty.

The inside of the Opera House also requires regular cleaning to keep it looking pristine. With millions of visitors passing through the Opera House each year, the floors, walls, and seats inside the building can quickly become dirty. To combat this, a dedicated team of cleaners works around the clock to maintain the interior. They vacuum carpets, polish wood surfaces, wipe down seats, and clean the glass windows that offer stunning views of Sydney Harbour.

One of the most challenging areas to keep clean inside the Opera House is the glass curtain walls. These enormous windows are made of thick, clear glass and allow natural light to flood into the building. While they provide beautiful views of the harbor, they also collect fingerprints, smudges, and dust. Specialized window cleaners are responsible for keeping these glass walls spotless. They use special tools, like long squeegees and eco-friendly cleaning solutions, to ensure the windows are always crystal clear.

The Opera House is also home to many areas that require delicate cleaning techniques due to the materials used in its construction. For example, the wooden panels inside the Concert Hall need to be carefully maintained so that they don't lose their shine. The wood adds warmth and beauty to the space, and its careful upkeep helps preserve the hall's excellent acoustics. The cleaners use soft cloths and gentle polishes to clean the wood without damaging it, ensuring that the materials stay in top condition.

The Opera House also has a team of conservationists who help with maintaining its historical and architectural integrity. Because the building is a UNESCO World Heritage site, great care must be taken to preserve its original design and materials. These experts monitor the building for any signs of wear or damage and make recommendations for how best to repair and maintain the structure without altering its iconic appearance.

In addition to cleaning the physical structure, the Opera House also implements green initiatives to reduce waste and promote sustainability. For example, the Opera House has switched to using environmentally friendly cleaning products that don't harm the building or the environment. The team also recycles as much waste as possible, including glass, paper, and plastic from the many events held at the Opera House. This commitment to sustainability ensures that the Opera House remains a beautiful and clean landmark for generations to come.

Another interesting fact about keeping the Sydney Opera House clean is that the job never really ends. The building is constantly exposed to the elements, so cleaning and maintenance are ongoing processes. The team of cleaners, conservationists, and maintenance workers is always busy making sure that the Opera House looks its best, both for the people of Sydney and for the millions of visitors who travel from all over the world to see it.

In conclusion, keeping the Sydney Opera House clean is no small task. From its gleaming white tiles to its massive glass windows and polished wooden interiors, every part of the Opera House requires special care and attention. The use of high-tech equipment like water jets, abseilers, and cleaning robots, along with a dedicated team of professionals, ensures that this world-famous landmark continues to sparkle. The work that goes into maintaining the Opera House is a testament to the pride that Australians and the world have in this architectural masterpiece. By keeping it clean and well-maintained, the Opera House continues to inspire awe and wonder in all who visit, standing tall as a shining symbol of beauty and creativity.

Chapter 18: The Sydney Opera House and the Olympics

The Sydney Opera House is one of Australia's most famous landmarks, known for its unique architecture and as a symbol of the country's vibrant culture. But did you know that the Opera House played an important role during the 2000 Summer Olympics in Sydney? The connection between the Opera House and the Olympics goes beyond being just a pretty backdrop for photographs—it became an iconic part of the celebrations and events that took place during this unforgettable global sporting event. The Opera House helped showcase Sydney's beauty to the world and served as a hub for special performances, ceremonies, and media coverage throughout the Olympics. Let's explore how this magnificent building became a part of Olympic history and how it helped make the Sydney Olympics one of the most memorable ever.

The 2000 Summer Olympics were a huge deal for Australia. It was the first time the country had hosted the Olympics since 1956, when the games were held in Melbourne. By the time Sydney was chosen as the host city for the 2000 Games, Australia was ready to show the world how much it had grown, both as a sporting nation and as a cultural hotspot. The Sydney Olympics were a massive event, with athletes and visitors from around the globe flocking to the city. The Opera House, being one of the most recognizable and beloved buildings in Australia, naturally became a central part of the Olympics.

One of the most magical aspects of the 2000 Olympics was how the entire city of Sydney came alive with Olympic spirit, and the Opera House was no exception. It was lit up with stunning lights and projections, making it an even more breathtaking sight. The famous white sails of the Opera House glowed with colors and images, symbolizing the diversity and unity of the athletes and countries participating in the Games. The projections included the Olympic rings, national flags, and scenes celebrating the world coming together in the spirit of friendly competition. This created a stunning visual that could be seen from across the harbor, capturing the attention of people all around the world who were watching the Olympics on TV.

In the weeks leading up to the Games, the Opera House also became a stage for cultural events and performances that helped build excitement. Sydney's vibrant arts scene took center stage, with performances of music, dance, and theater at the Opera House to celebrate the lead-up to the Olympics. These events were not only for the international visitors but also for the local Australians who were proud to be hosting such an important event. The Opera House, already a place where the arts thrived, became even more of a cultural hub during this time, bringing together people from all walks of life to enjoy world-class entertainment in the lead-up to the sporting events.

One of the most thrilling moments of the Sydney Olympics took place right at the Opera House: the passing of the Olympic torch. The Olympic torch relay is one of the most time-honored traditions of the Games. The torch is carried around the world by thousands of people, symbolizing peace, unity, and the passing of the Olympic spirit from one host city to the next. When the torch arrived in Sydney, it was carried past some of the city's most famous landmarks, and the Opera House was one of the key stops on its journey. As the torchbearer made their way to the steps of the Opera House, crowds gathered to watch this historic moment, cheering with excitement. The sight of the flame against the backdrop of the Opera House was unforgettable, and it became one of the most iconic images of the Sydney Olympics.

The Opera House wasn't just a pretty face during the Games—it was also an important venue for media coverage. Hundreds of journalists and media outlets from all over the world descended on Sydney to cover the Olympics, and many of them set up their broadcast stations near the Opera House. With the stunning harbor and the

Opera House as their backdrop, reporters shared news and updates about the Games with millions of viewers around the globe. It became the perfect spot for live broadcasts, as the iconic building added a touch of Australian culture and beauty to the coverage. The Opera House helped tell the story of the Sydney Olympics to the world, ensuring that its image would be forever linked to this historic event.

Even after the Games were over, the Opera House remained an important part of the celebrations. Once the competitions ended and the medals had been awarded, the city of Sydney erupted in celebration. The Opera House hosted many post-Olympic parties and events, bringing together athletes, dignitaries, and visitors to celebrate the success of the Games. It was a place for people to relax, enjoy the beauty of the harbor, and reflect on the incredible performances they had witnessed over the past few weeks. The Opera House continued to light up with colorful displays, keeping the festive Olympic spirit alive long after the closing ceremony.

The connection between the Sydney Opera House and the 2000 Olympics is a special one that remains in the memories of those who attended the Games or watched them on television. The Opera House didn't just serve as a backdrop—it became an active participant in the celebration, from hosting performances to being a key location for the Olympic torch relay. It symbolized the blending of culture and sport, showing the world that Sydney wasn't just a city of athletic talent but also a place where creativity and the arts flourished.

In the years since the Olympics, the Opera House continues to be a symbol of Australian pride. Every time there is a major event in Sydney, whether it's a sporting event, a festival, or a global celebration, the Opera House often plays a starring role. Its iconic design and cultural significance make it the perfect location for marking important moments, just as it did during the Sydney Olympics.

So, when you think about the Sydney Opera House, don't just picture it as a quiet place for concerts or plays—remember how it became a beacon of light and joy during one of the world's biggest sporting events. It wasn't just a building during the 2000 Summer Olympics; it was a symbol of Sydney's passion, energy, and love for the arts and sport. The Sydney Opera House and the Olympics will forever be linked in history, with both standing as reminders of a time when the world came together in celebration of human achievement. Whether it's through sport or the arts, the Opera House continues to inspire people from all over the globe, just as it did during the unforgettable Sydney 2000 Olympic Games.

Chapter 19: The Role of the Opera House in Tourism

The Sydney Opera House plays an incredibly important role in tourism, not only in Australia but also on a global scale. It is one of the most recognizable buildings in the world and has become a symbol of both Sydney and Australia as a whole. When people think about Australia, they often picture the white sails of the Opera House standing proudly on the edge of the harbor. This unique and stunning architectural masterpiece attracts millions of visitors every year, making it one of the busiest tourist destinations in the world. The role of the Opera House in tourism cannot be overstated, as it contributes not only to the economy but also to the cultural, social, and artistic life of Sydney. Its presence is felt far beyond the city limits, drawing visitors from every corner of the world.

For many tourists, the Sydney Opera House is at the very top of their list of places to visit when they come to Australia. The building itself is a wonder to behold, with its soaring white shells and its perfect location on the water's edge at Bennelong Point. The Opera House's stunning design makes it a must-see attraction for anyone interested in architecture, but it's more than just its appearance that draws visitors. The Opera House is home to countless performances, events, and experiences that make it a cultural hub for tourists and locals alike. Visitors can tour the building, watch performances, dine in world-class restaurants, and take part in special events throughout the year. This makes it a lively and dynamic destination, where there is always something happening to engage and excite tourists.

One of the key ways the Sydney Opera House contributes to tourism is by acting as a gateway to the city of Sydney. For many visitors, it's their first stop when they arrive in the city. The Opera House offers stunning views of Sydney Harbour, the Harbour Bridge, and the city skyline, making it the perfect place to start a sightseeing adventure. Tourists often spend hours walking around the Opera House, taking photos from every angle, and simply soaking in the beauty of the surroundings. It's not uncommon to see visitors from all over the world gathered around the Opera House, marveling at its design and taking in the breathtaking views of the harbor. Because of its location and significance, the Opera House has become a central part of the Sydney experience for tourists.

The Opera House is also a key driver of cultural tourism. It's not just a building to look at—it's a place where people come to experience world-class art and culture. The Opera House is home to a variety of performance companies, including Opera Australia, the Sydney Symphony Orchestra, and the Australian Ballet. It hosts hundreds of performances each year, from classical concerts and operas to contemporary music, theater, and dance. These performances attract art lovers from around the world who come to see some of the finest artists and performers in the world. Attending a performance at the Sydney Opera House is a bucket-list experience for many travelers, and the chance to see a live show in such an iconic venue is something that draws countless visitors every year.

In addition to its role as a performance venue, the Sydney Opera House also offers a range of tours and experiences designed specifically for tourists. Guided tours of the building are available in multiple languages, allowing visitors to learn about the history, architecture, and stories behind the Opera House. These tours take tourists behind the scenes, offering them a glimpse of areas of the building that are usually off-limits to the public, such as rehearsal spaces, backstage areas, and dressing rooms. For many tourists, these tours are a highlight of their trip, as they provide a deeper understanding of the Opera House's importance and the incredible work that goes on behind the scenes to create the performances seen on stage. The tours also give visitors the chance to learn more about the story of architect Jørn Utzon and the challenges that went into building the Opera House, which adds another layer of appreciation for the building's significance.

The Opera House is also home to a range of dining experiences, which add to its appeal as a tourist destination. Restaurants like Bennelong, which is located within the Opera House itself, offer world-class cuisine in an unbeatable setting. Tourists can enjoy fine dining while looking out over the harbor, creating a memorable and luxurious experience that adds to the Opera House's allure. There are also more casual dining options, such as Opera Bar, which provides a relaxed atmosphere where tourists can enjoy a drink or a meal while taking in the views of the Sydney Harbour Bridge and the water. These dining options help make the Opera House a full-day destination for many tourists, who can spend hours exploring, dining, and enjoying the scenery.

In addition to individual tourists, the Sydney Opera House is a major draw for large events and conventions. The Opera House regularly hosts conferences, business meetings, and corporate events, which bring international visitors to Sydney. These events often include performances or tours of the Opera House, adding to the overall experience for attendees. The building's status as a UNESCO World Heritage Site adds to its appeal for these types of events, as it offers a prestigious and unique venue for important gatherings. This, in turn, helps boost the city's economy by attracting international visitors who stay in hotels, dine in local restaurants, and explore other parts of Sydney during their visit.

The Opera House also plays a role in promoting Sydney as a destination for major international events. It is often featured in promotional materials, advertisements, and media coverage related to Sydney, making it a symbol of the city's appeal to tourists. Whether it's during New Year's Eve celebrations, which include fireworks launched from the harbor with the Opera House in the background, or during special events such as Vivid Sydney, the Opera House always takes center stage. Vivid Sydney, in particular, is a festival of light, music, and ideas that draws millions of tourists to the city. During the festival, the Opera House is illuminated with stunning light projections, turning the building into a canvas for artists from around the world. Events like these help keep the Opera House in the spotlight, ensuring that it remains a key driver of tourism for the city.

The Sydney Opera House's role in tourism goes beyond just attracting visitors to its doors—it helps promote Australia as a whole. The building is one of the most photographed landmarks in the world, and images of the Opera House are often used in advertising and marketing campaigns that promote Australia as a destination. The Opera House represents the modern, creative, and dynamic side of Australia, making it a symbol of the country's cultural and artistic achievements. When people see the Opera House, they immediately think of Australia, and this connection helps draw tourists to the country from all over the world. The Opera House has become an international icon, and its presence on the world stage helps boost Australia's profile as a must-visit destination for travelers.

In conclusion, the Sydney Opera House plays a critical role in tourism, not only for the city of Sydney but also for Australia as a whole. Its unique design, cultural significance, and stunning location make it a must-see destination for visitors from all over the world. The Opera House offers a wide range of experiences, from performances and tours to dining and events, ensuring that there is something for every type of tourist. Whether visitors are interested in architecture, art, history, or simply enjoying the beauty of Sydney Harbour, the Opera House provides an unforgettable experience that keeps tourists coming back year after year. As one of the most famous landmarks in the world, the Sydney Opera House continues to play a key role in promoting Australia to the rest of the world, ensuring that it remains a top destination for travelers of all ages.

Chapter 20: The Future of Sydney Opera House

The future of the Sydney Opera House is full of promise and excitement, as it continues to evolve as one of the world's most iconic cultural landmarks. Despite being over 50 years old, the Opera House is still a shining symbol of modern design and artistic innovation, but it's constantly looking forward to ensure it remains a leading hub for creativity, culture, and tourism. As the world around it changes, so too does the Opera House, making plans to adapt to new technology, expanding its role in global arts, improving its infrastructure, and ensuring it stays relevant for future generations.

One of the most important aspects of the future of the Sydney Opera House is its commitment to preserving and maintaining the building itself. The Opera House is a UNESCO World Heritage Site, meaning it's not only a vital part of Australia's heritage but also a landmark of global significance. Because of this, efforts are constantly underway to ensure that the structure remains in top condition for many years to come. This involves extensive restoration projects, upgrades, and improvements to the building's interior and exterior. These efforts are often invisible to the public, as they are carefully managed so that they don't disrupt the day-to-day activities at the Opera House, but they are essential for the long-term health of the building.

One of the major challenges the Opera House faces is maintaining its striking exterior, especially the famous white-tiled shells. While these sails make the building recognizable around the world, they also require a lot of care to stay clean and vibrant. The Opera House has already implemented regular maintenance schedules to keep the tiles in good condition, but future projects may focus on more advanced techniques for protecting and restoring the building's exterior. As technology advances, new methods for cleaning, preserving, and repairing architectural structures like the Opera House are being developed, and these innovations will likely play a key role in the future upkeep of the building.

In addition to physical maintenance, the Opera House is also preparing for the future by embracing new technology and digital advancements. The world of performing arts is changing rapidly, with digital experiences, virtual performances, and new forms of media becoming more common. The Sydney Opera House is committed to staying at the forefront of these changes, ensuring that it remains relevant in a world where technology plays an increasingly central role in how people experience art and entertainment. One of the ways the Opera House is doing this is by offering live-streamed performances, allowing people from all over the world to enjoy its shows without being physically present. This has already begun, but in the future, it's likely that the Opera House will continue to expand its digital offerings, perhaps even experimenting with virtual reality (VR) or augmented reality (AR) experiences.

The future of the Opera House also involves deepening its engagement with the local community and making it more accessible to everyone. While it's known as an international symbol of high culture, the Opera House wants to make sure that it remains a welcoming space for people from all walks of life. To achieve this, the Opera House is focused on developing programs that invite local audiences, including those from underrepresented communities, to engage with its performances, workshops, and events. This might include more free or low-cost performances, educational programs for young people, and events that celebrate the diversity of Sydney's population. By expanding its reach and making sure that everyone feels welcome, the Opera House is ensuring that it remains a vital part of Sydney's cultural fabric for many years to come.

Another exciting aspect of the future of the Sydney Opera House is its sustainability efforts. The Opera House is already working hard to reduce its environmental impact and become more eco-friendly, but future plans aim to take these efforts even further. As climate change becomes an increasingly urgent issue, the Opera House is committed to playing its part in protecting the planet. This means looking at how the building uses energy, how it manages waste, and how it can become more sustainable in its day-to-day operations. For example, the Opera House has already introduced LED lighting and upgraded its air conditioning systems to be more energy-efficient, but future efforts may focus on renewable energy sources, such as solar power, to reduce the building's carbon footprint even further. Additionally, the Opera House is exploring ways to make its food and beverage services more sustainable by reducing plastic waste and sourcing ingredients from local, sustainable producers.

In the future, the Opera House will likely expand its role as a center for innovation and collaboration. It has long been a place where artists from around the world come together to create groundbreaking performances, but the future will likely see even more partnerships and collaborations across different fields. This could involve new collaborations between artists, scientists, and technologists to create cutting-edge performances that blend art and technology in ways that we can't yet imagine. The Opera House's status as a global icon gives it the ability to attract some of the brightest and most creative minds from around the world, and the future may see it playing an even bigger role as a leader in the global arts community.

The Opera House is also focusing on future generations by continuing to invest in educational programs that inspire young people to engage with the arts. These programs range from workshops and school tours to performances designed specifically for young audiences. As part of its future plans, the Opera House will likely expand these educational offerings, using technology to reach even more young people and encouraging them to explore their creativity. By investing in the future of young artists and performers, the Opera House is ensuring that its legacy continues for many generations to come.

Looking ahead, the Sydney Opera House is also focused on its place in Sydney's growing tourism industry. As one of the city's most popular attractions, the Opera House plays a key role in attracting visitors from all over the world. The future of tourism is changing, with more emphasis on experiences and personal connections, and the Opera House is adapting to these trends. This could mean offering more interactive tours, creating personalized visitor experiences, or even developing new ways for tourists to engage with the building's history and architecture through digital tools like apps or virtual guides. Whatever form it takes, the Opera House will continue to be a key driver of tourism in Sydney, offering unforgettable experiences to visitors from around the world.

Finally, the future of the Sydney Opera House involves its role in shaping Australian culture. The Opera House has always been a symbol of Australia's creativity, boldness, and willingness to embrace the new and innovative. As Australia's cultural landscape continues to evolve, the Opera House will remain a leader in showcasing the best of Australian talent, while also bringing in international artists and performers to share their work with Australian audiences. It will continue to be a place where different cultures, ideas, and traditions come together, fostering a spirit of inclusivity and collaboration that defines Australia's cultural identity.

In conclusion, the future of the Sydney Opera House is one filled with growth, innovation, and a deep commitment to preserving its legacy while adapting to the needs and challenges of a changing world. Whether through new technological advancements, sustainability efforts, community engagement, or continued excellence in the arts, the Opera House is poised to remain a global cultural landmark for generations to come. As it looks ahead, the Sydney Opera House is focused on ensuring that it continues to inspire, entertain, and connect people from all over the world, just as it has done for more than five decades. The future promises exciting new possibilities, and the Opera House is ready to embrace them while staying true to its iconic heritage.

Epilogue

As we come to the end of our journey through the Sydney Opera House, we hope you've discovered just how special this place truly is. From its daring design to its role as a stage for some of the world's greatest performances, the Opera House is a symbol of creativity, culture, and adventure. It's not just a building—it's a piece of history that continues to inspire people from all over the world.

By now, you've learned about the amazing vision of Jørn Utzon, the incredible challenges faced during construction, and the way the Opera House has become a beacon of Australian pride. But the story doesn't end here! The Sydney Opera House is still alive with excitement, hosting events, concerts, and festivals that bring people together to celebrate the arts. It continues to grow and change, just like the city of Sydney itself.

The next time you see a picture of this iconic landmark or, if you're lucky enough, visit it in person, you'll know the rich history behind those gleaming sails. You'll understand that it's more than just a beautiful building—it's a place where stories come to life, where dreams take shape, and where the future is always bright.

So, as you turn the last page, remember that every landmark has a story, and sometimes, that story is still being written. The Sydney Opera House is one of those places, and now you're a part of its story too! Thanks for joining us on this exciting adventure. Who knows what incredible places we'll explore next?

The End.